WRITING IN NURSING

BRIEF GUIDES TO WRITING IN THE DISCIPLINES

EDITED BY
THOMAS DEANS, *University of Connecticut*
MYA POE, *Northeast University*

Although writing-intensive courses across the disciplines are now common at many colleges and universities, few books meet the precise needs of those offerings. These books do. Compact, candid, and practical, the *Brief Guides to Writing in the Disciplines* deliver experience-tested lessons and essential writing resources for those navigating fields ranging from Biology and Engineering to Music and Political Science.

Authored by experts in the field who also have a knack for teaching, these books introduce students to discipline-specific writing habits that seem natural to insiders but still register as opaque to those new to a major or to specialized research. Each volume offers key writing strategies backed by crisp explanations and examples; each anticipates the missteps that even bright newcomers to a specialized discourse typically make; and each addresses the irksome details that faculty get tired of marking up in student papers.

For faculty accustomed to teaching their own subject matter but not writing, these books provide a handy vocabulary for communicating what good academic writing is and how to achieve it. Most of us learn to write through trial and error, often over many years, but struggle to impart those habits of thinking and writing to our students. The *Brief Guides to Writing in the Disciplines* make both the central lessons and the field-specific subtleties of writing explicit and accessible.

These versatile books will be immediately useful for writing-intensive courses but should also prove an ongoing resource for students as they move through more advanced courses, on to capstone research experiences, and even into their graduate studies and careers.

OTHER AVAILABLE TITLES IN THIS SERIES INCLUDE:

Writing in Anthropology: *A Brief Guide*
Shan-Estelle Brown
(ISBN: 9780199381319)

Writing in Engineering: *A Brief Guide*
Robert Irish
(ISBN: 9780199343553)

Writing in Political Science: *A Brief Guide*
Mika LaVaque-Manty and Danielle LaVaque-Manty
(ISBN: 9780190203931)

Writing in Sociology: *A Brief Guide*
Cary Moskovitz and Lynn Smith-Lovin
(ISBN: 9780190203924)

Writing in Biology: *A Brief Guide*
Leslie Ann Roldan and Mary-Lou Pardue
(ISBN: 9780199342716)

WRITING IN NURSING

A BRIEF GUIDE

Thomas Lawrence Long
Cheryl Tatano Beck
UNIVERSITY OF CONNECTICUT

Oxford University Press
New York

Oxford University Press is a department of the University of Oxford.
It furthers the University's objective of excellence in research, scholarship,
and education by publishing worldwide. Oxford is a registered trade mark
of Oxford University Press in the UK and certain other countries.

Published in the United States of America by Oxford University Press
198 Madison Avenue, New York, NY 10016, United States of America.

Library of Congress Cataloging-in-Publication Data

Names: Long, Thomas Lawrence, author. | Beck, Cheryl Tatano, author.
Title: Writing in nursing : a brief guide / Thomas Lawrence Long, Cheryl Tatano Beck.
Other titles: Brief guides to writing in the disciplines.
Description: New York : Oxford University Press, [2017] | Series: Brief
    guides to writing in the disciplines | Includes bibliographical references.
Identifiers: LCCN 2016040842| ISBN 9780190202231 | ISBN 9780190635022
Subjects: | MESH: Writing | Nurses' Instruction
Classification: LCC RT24 | NLM WZ 345 | DDC 808.06/661--dc23 LC record
available at https://lccn.loc.gov/2016040842

BRIEF TABLE OF CONTENTS

TABLE OF CONTENTS

CHAPTER 2 **Getting Started: Identifying
a Clinical Problem and Evaluating
the Research Literature   20**

CHAPTER 7 **Advocacy Writing, Clinical
Practice Guidelines/Articles,
and Conference Proposals   112**

CHAPTER 8 **Thinking and Communicating
Visually: Tables, Figures,
Presentation Slides,
and Posters   134**

PREFACE

Most nurses enter their profession because they feel a calling to care for people's health and well-being, not because they love writing. Yet along the way most discover—either while in school or later on the job—that they need to be effective written communicators.

We love writing. We love what it can do. We love the intellectual, personal, and professional challenges and rewards that writing provides. But we also know that writing entails very hard work.

Between us we have a combined nearly sixty years of full-time teaching experience in higher education at community colleges, at state universities, at private colleges, and now at a public research university. One of us (Thomas Lawrence Long) is a professor of English in a school of nursing who provides writing support services to nursing students and faculty and who is experienced as a technical editor and teacher of technical writing. He has dozens of books, book chapters, and articles to his credit. The other (Cheryl Tatano Beck) is Board of Trustees Distinguished Professor of nursing who uses qualitative and quantitative methods to study postpartum mood and anxiety disorders and who has published award winning textbooks on nursing research. In addition, she has published or edited several books and published scores of research articles. Our success as writers has come after years of practice, learning from our professors and other writers, and revising (often many times) our own writing with the guidance of editors.

Both of us have taught undergraduate and graduate nursing students in writing-intensive courses. We understand that students struggle with academic writing and, later in their careers, struggle to get a handle on nursing's modes of professional communication. In this brief guide we offer the essentials of getting started in nursing writing.

In order to write this book we have gone beyond our personal experiences by consulting our colleagues here in the University of Connecticut's School of Nursing, as well as nursing faculty and editors who are members of the International Academy of Nurse Editors. Various anonymous reviewers who are experts in writing instruction and in nursing education have also given us suggestions after reading earlier drafts of this book, as well as the editors of this book series, Tom Deans (University of Connecticut) and Mya Poe (Northeastern University).

This guide to writing in nursing is based on three fundamental concepts:

- *Writing is not a simple container for thoughts, information, and ideas.* To write like a nurse, one has to think like a nurse. Writing is a form of thinking. For this reason we spend a lot of space in this book describing how nurses and nurse scientists think. Most students encounter writing instruction in English courses. However, the ways of thinking, the word choices, the formats, and the structures of nursing writing are very different from those in an English course. In a real sense, one has to relearn how to write for nursing.
- *Writing is not a simple transferable skill.* Professors often mistakenly assume that, once students have taken a first-year writing course, they should know how to apply writing skills in every situation. But it is not that easy.

Writing depends on context. Nurses and nurse scientists constitute what's called a *discourse community*; there are recognizable ways of thinking and writing that are characteristic of nurses. In nursing school one learns how to think like a nurse and apply clinical judgment like a nurse, but also how to communicate like a nurse. Just as with clinical skills and clinical judgment, learning to write like a nurse doesn't happen overnight or even in one semester.

- *Writing to learn, and learning to write.* This brief guide to nursing writing acknowledges that some writing assignments are designed to help students think more deeply and critically about clinical practice (*writing to learn*). At the same time, we introduce some of the genres (modes or formats or types of writing) that are typical of academic and professional nursing so that both students and practitioners handle them with skill and confidence (*learning to write*). Examples of these include case studies, literature reviews, poster presentations, and advocacy writing.

We presume that writing takes time, effort, and practice, just as do nursing clinical skills and judgment.

In Chapter 1, we explain that nurses' writing is effective when they pay attention to their personal credibility, give the reader reasons to care about their topics, and demonstrate their professional competence. We also explain the dynamics of nursing research and evidence-based practice, as well as briefly introducing the clinical, academic, and professional genres that this guide will cover.

The second chapter helps writers identify a clinical problem or opportunity for improvement and then to evaluate the published research literature (the evidence base) in order to understand both what we know and what we don't know about a phenomenon. Identifying a clinical problem is the starting point for nursing writing, but we will show how to move beyond personal observations in order to understand the phenomenon more fully.

In the next two chapters we explain different kinds of clinical writing. Clinical reflective writing (Chapter 3) focuses on thinking deeply and professionally about critical clinical encounters. Clinical reflective writing isn't considered professional writing because it is more typically used in a curriculum to encourage certain habits of thought, so it's what we are calling *writing to learn*. Chapter 4 explains how to write clinical case studies, an academic assignment that analyzes in even greater depth encounters like the ones taken up in clinical reflection papers. It might also be something that nurses develop professionally for publication. In either case, the clinical case study moves beyond personal reflections by synthesizing the research literature.

Chapters 5 and 6 explain two forms of academic writing: research critiques and literature reviews. While a research critique provides a focused analysis and evaluation of one published research article, a literature review examines several. A research critique is another example of writing to learn, an assignment that sharpens one's skill as a consumer of nursing research. A literature review, however, is a signature genre for academic writing in nursing, providing a foundation to inform evidence-based practice and to establish more advanced research projects.

In Chapter 7 we explain forms of professional writing that reach out to wider audiences. Many nurses want to express informed opinions about an important or controversial topic or to persuade wider audiences to adopt their view through publishing letters to the editor or op-ed essays. Many of our students have done so successfully. Later in their careers, nurses may want to contribute to the clinical practice literature. And increasingly graduate students and even undergraduates are invited to submit proposals for presenting posters at conferences.

The final chapters of the book guide readers in some of technical aspects of writing in nursing: using visuals, presentation slides, and posters (Chapter 8); using language professionally and effectively (Chapter 9); and synthesizing and citing sources in American Psychological Association (APA) style (Chapter 10).

Nursing students and registered nurses have important observations to make about health, illness, and health policy, and others need to read what they write. Our hope is that this brief guide will be a trusted companion on their journeys through nursing programs and into the profession.

ABOUT THE AUTHORS

THOMAS LAWRENCE LONG, PHD, is associate professor in residence in the University of Connecticut's School of Nursing, where he provides writing support services in the Center for Nursing Scholarship. Jointly appointed in the Women's, Gender, and Sexuality Studies Program, he publishes research on literary and cultural representations of health, sexuality, and health professions.

CHERYL TATANO BECK, DNSc, CNM, FAAN, is a University of Connecticut Distinguished Professor jointly appointed to the School of Nursing and School of Medicine. Her groundbreaking qualitative and quantitative research into postpartum mood disorders and traumatic childbirth has made a significant contribution to improving the care provided to new mothers. Her book-length treatments of nursing research and postpartum mental health have won the *American Journal of Nursing* Book of the Year Awards and have educated a generation of undergraduate and graduate nursing students. She is a Fellow of the American Academy of Nursing.

ACKNOWLEDGMENTS

We are grateful for the patience of family, friends, and colleagues during the labor and delivery of this book. The staff of the University of Connecticut's School of Nursing and its Center for Nursing Scholarship have given us indispensable support. What we know about writing we have learned from our teachers, mentors, colleagues, and editors. What we know about teaching academic and professional writing we have learned from our students and colleagues. We are also grateful to our students who allowed us to publish in this book excerpts of their work for our courses. Our thanks go to all of them.

WRITING IN NURSING

CREDIBILITY, CARE, AND COMPETENCE IN NURSING WRITING

For me, writing and nursing are inseparable—each informs the other.... Writing continually informs nursing by preserving our stories.... nurses and writers are equally watchful and precise—always looking for what others perhaps don't see while anticipating three or four strides down the road. I've been told that my writing conveys compassion, but with detachment. As a nurse, this duality is also necessary.

—Stacy Nigliazzo (2015)

Writing is not a container for thinking or a simple transferable skill. Writing is a form of thinking. To write well is to think well.

In this chapter we explain the thinking of nursing science and practice to show you the relationship between thinking like a nurse and writing like a nurse. We survey the concepts of *translational science* and *evidence-based practice* and introduce you to basic terminology about writing. Finally, we briefly explain some of the common genres—that is, the types of writing and communication—you will encounter in your academic and professional careers.

Thinking Like a Nurse: Key Concepts

Translational Science: From Bench to Bedside

Scientists in physical sciences like chemistry and physics or life sciences like biology are often motivated by basic curiosity about physical or natural phenomena. We give them some measure of latitude in exploring their specialization without someone asking, "So what?" Scientific curiosity is an intrinsic good. However, in health sciences like nursing, research is all about the "So what?" Nurses research phenomena that make a difference in improving people's health and are always concerned with the implications for nursing practice. As a consequence, nursing science and its clinical applications are called *translational science*, "translating" basic or "bench" science discoveries (either literally at the lab bench or in a clinical setting) into clinical applications (at the patient's bedside).

Basic research's purpose is to increase knowledge through systematically investigating a phenomenon. In health sciences, bench research can involve examining physiologic processes at different levels such as molecules, cells, tissues, or organs (Grady, 2010), as well as health and disease among patient populations.

Translational research moves scientific results from the laboratory to clinical practice in order to improve patient care. Nurse scientists' translational studies can focus on identifying barriers, facilitating knowledge adoption, predicting of organizational adherence to evidence-based practice (EBP) guidelines, and evaluating clinicians' attitudes toward EBP (Titler, 2010).

Throughout your nursing education you will be using published translational research to inform your writing, so it's important for you to understand it and how it is produced. Translational science is not a linear, unidirectional process but rather a dynamic bidirectional process with complex feedback

Translational Science vs. Evidence-Based Practice

Translational science is different from evidence-based practice. In translational science, researchers study how health care workers and systems could (or should) adopt practices that align with what the scientific evidence tells us. Evidence-based practice, on the other hand, focuses on how health care workers and systems actually apply scientific evidence in their practices (Titler, 2010). Parsing such distinctions may seem worlds away from writing, but in fact most of your writing assignments will ask you—explicitly or implicitly—to synthesize translational science and show how it could inform clinical practice. Given this translational orientation, the best nurses are almost always asking as they write, "How does my writing contribute to advancing patient care?"

loops. These two directions are (1) the continuous development and reevaluation of an intervention in various settings and for differing populations, and (2) the active integration of findings from different clinical settings into developing new basic and applied research studies (Grady, 2010).

Evidence-Based Practice

As Barnsteiner, Reeder, Palma, Preston, and Walton (2010) remind us, "Excellence in clinical practice is not a static, finite achievement but a continual pursuit to adapt emerging knowledge to the practice setting and the individual needs of the patient and the family" (p. 225). EBP is the conscientious use of the best evidence that is currently available in making decisions regarding the care of patients (Sackett et al., 2000).

In other words, EBP means that nurses' clinical expertise and patients' preferences are integrated with the best translational research evidence in clinical decision making. EBP is not a cookbook practice but instead involves personalizing the research evidence to fit patients' specific circumstances.

You will use EBP thinking about patients and clinical phenomena in all your nursing courses and in the writing for those courses. Sometimes you will employ EBP thinking in informal writing (like journals or reflection papers) while at other times you will engage in EBP thinking in formal academic writing (like research article critiques or literature reviews). But whether you're being asked to write formally or informally, keep in mind *evidence* as a key term. That evidence could be a written narrative of what happened at your clinical site (in a case study), or it might be a peer-reviewed research study.

The Steps of Evidence-Based Practice

According to Melnyk and Fineout-Overholt (2011), the six steps of EBP are:

1. Ask the burning clinical question,
2. Search for and collect the most relevant and best evidence,
3. Critically appraise the evidence,
4. Integrate all evidence with one's clinical expertise, patient preferences, and values in making a practice decision or change,
5. Evaluate outcomes of the practice decision or change based on evidence,
6. Disseminate the outcomes of the EBP decision or change. (p. 9)

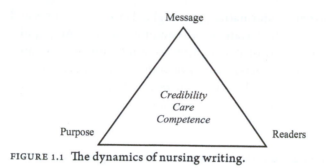

FIGURE 1.1 The dynamics of nursing writing.

In either case, your job as a writer is to connect such evidence to a claim for a certain kind of practice.

Writing Like a Nurse: Key Concepts

You have something you want to say. You have a reason for writing. You have readers in mind. Even in a writing assignment for a course, you have ideas or information that you want to convey (a *message*). You have a *purpose* in writing (which might be simply to earn a good grade, or it might be to make a persuasive argument or to alert people to a health problem). And someone will read what you've written (your professor in a course, or other nursing students, or health professionals, or the general audience of a daily newspaper). At the heart of your writing, however, is that you need to demonstrate your credibility as a writer, to engage your readers' interests so that they will care about your topic, and to demonstrate your competence as a nurse and writer.

Message

Nurses' writing includes information and analysis. In papers for a course you might describe a patient's condition or a disease process. You might summarize epidemiological data concerning disease and the populations most affected. But beyond summarizing information, you might also analyze causes and effects (e.g., why certain health conditions affect some populations disproportionately or why certain treatments are more effective than others). How you craft that message, however, will depend as much on your purpose in writing and the readers for whom you're writing as on anything else.

Purpose

While you are a student, your most basic purpose is pretty simple: You want to earn a good grade on the writing assignment to pass the course! However, as you become more deeply involved in the nursing profession and later in your career, your purposes will become more complex. Some of the likely purposes for which you will use written communication include the following:

- Demonstrate your knowledge and understanding of a health problem or professional issue.
- Define the evidence base concerning a health issue and analyze its implications for nursing practice.
- Learn and think more deeply and more critically about a clinical phenomenon or problem.
- Propose a solution to a clinical problem or a policy issue.

Keep in mind the relationship between readers and purpose. Even when you think of yourself as mostly informing your readers, you are also implicitly trying to persuade them that the information is important and that you are its credible source. Even in your writing assignments for courses, you are trying to persuade your professors that you have carefully searched and selected the literature, that you have diligently prepared your paper, and that you know what you are talking about. As you consider your readers in relation to purposes, consider the following questions:

- To what extent are you trying to *inform* your readers?
- To what extent are you trying to *persuade* your readers?
- To what extent are your readers seeking help or information?
- To what extent are your readers seeking a persuasive argument on a clinical practice or policy issue?

Readers

Different readers have different expectations and different needs from your written communication. Professional readers (like nursing faculty and fellow nursing students), for example, have expectations about the form of your writing (the genre), the ways that you use language (style), and the kinds of sources and information that you use (evidence). Later in your nursing career, non-expert readers will need you to explain complex health phenomena in non-technical language and, in some instances, to be aware that they have limited literacy or limited English proficiency. As you think about your readers, consider the following questions:

- Are your readers your professors, your fellow students, both, or an imagined audience outside the classroom?
- How much do they know about your topic?
- Are they interested in your topic and are they hostile, neutral, or friendly to your point of view on the topic?
- What are the specifications (expectations) for the writing assignment that you are undertaking?
- What do your readers expect from your style or format of presentation?
- What do they want your writing to do for them?

Credibility, Care, Competence

Beyond readers and purpose, nursing writing is also about *credibility, care,* and *competence.* Through your writing you are establishing your personal *credibility*, getting the audience to *care* emotionally about the topic, and demonstrating your technical *competence* through clear arguments and reliable evidence.

Credibility

While you are a nursing student, you are beginning to invest in something that will pay dividends throughout your career: your professional reputation. Whether it is the time and attention you invest in a case study, a research critique, or a literature review, you are building a reputation with your professors and fellow students. Later as a professional nurse, you will extend those skills to your nursing practice. Just as people put their trust in you when you demonstrate yourself to be a knowledgeable, caring, and well-prepared nurse in clinical practice, so they will put their trust in you when you are writing for them.

You can cultivate credibility over time by demonstrating consistently that you are knowledgeable, caring, and well prepared. Consider the following:

- Do you have a reputation for being someone who is prepared in advance for academic or clinical assignments?
- Do you have a reputation for being someone whose work is careful, complete, and detailed?

In your writing you can establish your credibility by the thoroughness of your literature search, the care with which you synthesize the literature, and even your attention to the mechanical details of a paper's format. Even something as conventional as a methods section of a research paper provides you with an opportunity to demonstrate your thoroughness and credibility. Above all you should be thinking of the question: *Why should readers trust me and pay attention to me?*

Consider the following example in which the author explains not just what he did but why he made certain methodological choices. He also acknowledges limitations and discusses the process he used to correct for potential limitations in his research process:

In a March 2013 survey of epidemiological literature concerning oral sex as a vector of HIV transmission, the author conducted a literature search of PubMed using keywords ("oral sex," "HIV transmission," "MSM or "men who have sex with men," "fellatio," "oral practices," "oral sex") and MeSH (medical subject heading) terms (including ["HIV Infections/transmission"] OR ["HIV Seropositivity/transmission"; ["Mouth" OR "Mouth Diseases" OR "Mouth Mucosa"]; ["Men's Health" OR "Homosexuality, Male"]). The author discovered that there is a not a MeSH term for "oral sex" or "MSM" (the less stigmatizing term than "gay" and more accurate for research purposes since it describes a behavior rather than an identity and recognizes the reality that many men do not identify themselves as gay even though their sexual activity is significantly involved with other men). The author conducted similar searches in other health science databases: the Cumulative Index to Nursing and Allied Health Literature (CINAHL) and Cochrane Database of Systematic Reviews, as well as the general science indexes, Web of Science and Scopus. This search identified 71 articles published between 1988 and 2013. The author selected 11 representative research articles (7 systematic reviews, 2 laboratory and/or clinical studies, 1 case study of 75 HIV infected men, 1 hypothesis analysis) from the literature published since 1998, in other words, over the past 15 years (nearly half the published history of the epidemic).

Through the kind of detail the author above provided in his literature search, you, too, can demonstrate credibility to readers that you have done a thorough job of searching and synthesizing the literature. However, you also need to connect emotionally with your readers.

Care

Effective writing also acknowledges that readers respond when the writer engages them affectively (that is, emotionally). The nursing profession takes pride in cultivating professional values of caring, with considerable thought having been given to theories of nursing care. However, we cannot take for granted that our personal passions will be those of our readers. We need to help the reader to answer this question: *Why should I care about what you have to say?*

In 1999 the Association of Women's Health, Obstetrics, and Neonatal Nurses (AWHONN) asked Cheryl Beck to write a monograph based on her research program. The monograph, *Postpartum Mood and Anxiety Disorders: Case Studies, Research, and Nursing Care,* is now in its third edition (Beck, 2014). Nurses who are members of AWHONN can earn continuing education units by reading this monograph.

Depending on the style of the document, there are a variety of ways of emotionally engaging your reader:

Use a striking or eloquent quotation or a quotation from a respected source

As a qualitative researcher whose data are the words of her patient participants, Cheryl Beck often employs this device, as she did in this example from a study of traumatic childbirth (Beck, 2004a, p. 32):

> As Lisa recalled, "I am amazed that three and a half hours in the labor and delivery room could cause such utter destruction in my life. It truly was like being a victim of a violent crime or rape."

Appeal to the significance to nursing
For example, as one of our students wrote in a course paper:

> As HIV becomes more of a chronic illness and less of a "death sentence" more and more women with HIV infection are having babies. Care for these women requires special attention, including monitoring of T-cells and viral load results and prescribing of HIV antiretroviral medications with considerable side effects. There is always the risk of a baby being born with HIV despite all our interventions. There is also the risk of future unknown side effects to the child from medications provided during pregnancy. There are few data describing the experience of the nurse practitioner, particularly the HIV specialist nurse practitioner, who provides outpatient care for HIV infected pregnant women.

Provide readers with startling or surprising data
For example, as another of our students wrote in a paper:

> In the United States today, 5.4 million people have Alzheimer's disease, including one in every eight Americans over the age of 65 (Alzheimer's Association, 2012). Alzheimer's disease is the leading cause of dementia.

Worldwide, it is estimated that 24.3 million people have dementia, expected to increase to 81.1 million by the year 2040 (Ferri et al., 2005).

Demonstrate your personal experience, expertise, or engagement with an issue

One of our graduate students, who returned to school after spending many years in clinical practice, wrote in one of her papers:

> As an intrapartum nurse in a large suburban teaching hospital I have witnessed many trends over the past 20 years. There has been the desire for natural childbirth, the increased use of epidural anesthesia for labor, the decision to attempt to VBAC (vaginal birth after cesarean), the decline of VBACs, and the latest: the maternal request for a nonmedically indicated cesarean birth. This latest trend is sometimes referred to as a "cesarean on demand." None of the previous trends have perplexed me as much as the cesarean on demand.

Competence

Finally, an effective writer demonstrates competence by having a cogent argument supported by reliable evidence. In a world confused by false health claims and seemingly contradictory health research study findings, we must demonstrate a reasonable weighing of evidence and a cautious assertion of claims.

In this book when we discuss logic and evidence and when we discuss the available means of informing and persuading audiences, we will use the word *argument*. While *argument* can mean a heated or angry discussion, we are using it in a more technical sense: using logic and evidence to make a point, to persuade readers, or to inform them about improving health outcomes.

Depending on the style of the document, there are a variety of ways of demonstrating your competence.

Acknowledge and explain differences of opinion or definitional ambiguities

For example, from a student's paper on nursing burnout:

> Numerous proposed definitions provided by popular researchers share mostly similar ideas of what that definition could be. According to Weiler (1990) burnout is a "collapse of the human spirit." Pines and Maslach (1978) define burnout as "a syndrome of physical and emotional exhaustion involving the development of a negative self-concept, negative job attitude and loss of concern and feeling for clients." For the purposes of this paper nursing burnout will be defined as: "a syndrome of emotional exhaustion, depersonalization, and lack of personal accomplishment" (Wunderlich, 1996).

Explain nursing science's implications for nursing practice

As the same student has written in the conclusion of his policy paper on nursing burnout:

> The most significant piece to the solution of solving the burnout crisis is to find a clinical definition for what burnout is. Once a definition is devised, burnout can be measured and treated more accurately. Because burnout is a long-term problem starting with nurse symptoms of feeling exhausted and ending with the nurse leaving his/her job, preventative measures might be more effective than

treatment measures. The best solution to a long-term ill-ness is preventing the factors that cause the illness. It is no different in the solution to burnout.

Signature Genres of Writing in Nursing

Not all the writing you will do in college nursing courses maps neatly onto professional practice. Some of the writing that you will be assigned by your professors is designed to help you master course content and think more deeply about nursing science and practice. Other writing assignments teach you the kinds of genres practiced by advanced academic nursing writ-ers and professional nurses in clinical practice.

Because you will undertake a variety of writing assign-ments in your nursing curriculum, we identify the most common types or genres of writing in academic nursing: clini-cal reflective writing and case studies, research critiques, and literature reviews. Some of the genres we briefly introduce in this chapter are designed to help you learn more deeply and critically about a topic, but they are not used in clinical prac-tice. Moreover, honors students and graduate students are fre-quently encouraged to disseminate their research findings, in conference presentations, scholarly research journals, and clinical professional journals.

We structure this guide around three categories of writing: *clinical* genres, *academic* genres, and *professional* genres. Table 1.1 maps how these genres are related to your audiences and purposes.

Clinical Genres: Reflective Writing and Case Studies

During your clinical courses and later in your nursing practice, certain experiences with patients will stand out, perhaps because of the unusual nature of a patient's health condition or the complexities of the patient's circumstances. Clinical

TABLE 1.1 **Connecting Purposes, Audience, and Genres**

Purposes	Audiences	Genres
Identify and describe a clinical phenomenon.	Professors, nurses, fellow nursing students	*Clinical*: Clinical reflective writing, case studies *Academic*: Literature reviews *Professional*: Clinical practice articles
Summarize, evaluate, synthesize the evidence base and identify gaps.	Professors, nurses, conference participants	*Academic*: Research critiques, literature reviews, poster presentations
Propose a research project or an evidence-based practice change.	Health professionals, general lay readers, conference organizers, administrators of health institutions	*Academic*: Research proposals *Professional*: Advocacy writing, proposal abstracts, evidence-based clinical practice guidelines

genres, such as reflective writing and case studies, invite you to reflect deeply and critically about clinical encounters.

Reflective writing

Reflective writing is an effective practice to help you think deeply and critically. Through reflective writing you purposely contemplate your thoughts and feelings regarding a significant clinical experience: "Writing makes our thoughts visible, laying it open for us to modify, extend, develop or critique" (Usher, Tollefson, & Francis, 2001, p. 16).

Case studies

Case studies are descriptions of a single case that has unique characteristics. In addition to describing, a case study should also interpret and explain various aspects of care (Aitken & Marshall, 2007). In writing a case study you present the clinical decision making that occurred throughout a patient's care.

Along with summarizing the past care, you include new insights into future nursing care.

Academic Genres: Research Critiques and Literature Reviews

As a nursing student, academic genres, such as *research critiques* and *literature reviews,* focus your attention in ways that lead you to analyze and synthesize the published evidence in order to show how it applies to clinical practice.

Research critiques

Research critiques are used to help you think more deeply and critically about nursing research, enabling you to become a more knowledgeable consumer of nursing scholarship. In a research critique you provide a critical appraisal of a single research study, assessing the study's strengths as well as its weaknesses. Writing a research critique helps you to cultivate critical thinking and helps you to apply the newly acquired knowledge learned in your courses.

Literature reviews

Literature reviews are one of the signature genres of nursing research, identifying a phenomenon, synthesizing the state of nursing knowledge, and deriving implications for nursing practice or research. There are two senses of the term *review of the literature* or *literature review.* In the first sense, a *review of the literature* appears as a section of a longer research proposal, poster presentation, or research article. As a component of a proposal, poster, or article, the review of the literature summarizes what is known about a phenomenon in order to provide background to the contribution that you plan to propose or that you have made already in conducting a research article. In the second sense, however, a *literature review* means a standalone genre that identifies a research question, employs specific literature search methods, explains those methods, analyzes and synthesizes what the published literature reveals, and draws implications for clinical practice or further research.

Professional Genres: Advocacy Writing, Clinical Practice Guidelines, Clinical Practice Articles, Conference Presentations

Outside of a classroom or other academic setting, you will find that your nursing career provides occasions when your skills as a writer will allow you to exercise leadership as a health professional and to educate patients and other health information consumers. In particular, you will need to be an *advocate* on behalf of the nursing profession or of vulnerable populations, whose concerns you will address in advocacy writing. Moreover, in clinical practice articles, practice guidelines, and professional presentations and publications you will communicate with other professionals about important nursing issues.

Advocacy writing

Advocacy writing includes genres such as editorials and court testimony that allow nurses to share important knowledge and insightful opinions about a range of topics: health care systems; health professions; health maintenance; and the well-being of pregnant women, children, the poor, the elderly, and other vulnerable populations. Your voice needs to be heard whether you express yourself in a letter to the editor, an editorial in a professional journal, an op-ed essay in a mass publication, or prepared remarks and testimony at a formal public hearing.

Early in your clinical career you will probably be expected to do little workplace writing. At a time of growing use of electronic medical records (with on-screen checkboxes and pull-down options) you may not even do much writing in full sentences and paragraphs to provide comments in patients' charts. However, over the course of your career, you will find yourself in situations where you are called upon to prepare a variety of documents, such as *clinical practice guidelines* and *clinical practice articles*.

Clinical practice guidelines

Clinical practice guidelines are "a set of recommendations for care of a patient population that is issued by a professional association, leading healthcare center, or government organization. Guidelines are not agency-specific" (Brown, 2012, p. 8). Evidence-based clinical practice guidelines are adapted to an agency-specific clinical protocol, which provides specific actions for nurses in providing care at that health care agency. Clinical practice guidelines are developed from systematic reviews of findings from individual studies on a topic. The audience for a clinical practice article is nurses in clinical practice who care for patients at the bedside.

Clinical practice articles

Clinical practice articles allow nurses to share with other clinical nurses a fresh understanding of patient needs and nursing care regarding a particular health phenomenon. Like a case study, the idea for writing a clinical practice article may come from your own experience providing care to a patient and the patient's family. The clinical practice article might focus on a nursing intervention that was extremely successful or maybe one that was frustrating. You might also highlight issues that you encountered in providing nursing care and how you resolved those issues.

Presentations

Presentations can be given to expert audiences, such as other nurses and physicians, or non-expert audiences, such as patients, families and advocates. Eventually, you may find yourself interested in taking on leadership roles within your health care agency or professional organizations. You may also decide to work toward administrative, managerial, and even executive roles, all of which will require you to hone your skills as an oral and written communicator.

Because nursing students and clinical nurses also give presentations at state, regional, and national professional conferences, they need to write *conference proposal abstracts*. If they wish to be invited to present at a conference, nursing students need to submit a winning proposal abstract, and we will explain how to write those. And if invited to a conference, you may need to create a *poster presentation*, which we will cover in our chapter on visuals.

In this book we limit ourselves to significant, high-impact forms of professional writing. Below we list several more kinds of writing that you are likely to use in your nursing career but that we can't cover in our brief guide:

- Care plans
- E-mails
- Memos
- Required official forms
- Medical record narratives
- Communication with physicians and other health professionals
- Résumé and job application letter
- Formal proposals (policy or practice change documents)
- Health information for patients (brochures, presentations)

GETTING STARTED

Identifying a Clinical Problem and
Evaluating the Research Literature

Over 150 years ago, the founder of modern professional nursing, Florence Nightingale, remarked:

> The most important practical lesson that can be given to nurses is to teach them what to observe—how to observe—what symptoms indicate improvement—what the reverse—which are of importance—which are of none—which are the evidence of neglect—and of what kind of neglect. All this is what ought to make part, and an essential part, of the training of every nurse.

Watch. Listen. Pay attention. Ask questions. Those basic habits of nurses are still central to your practice today and, as we argue here, to your writing.

Previously we have described two signature patterns of thinking found in nursing's technical and scientific writing: translational science and evidence-based practice. As a student, some of your writing assignments will involve:

1. Identifying a clinical problem for practice or research
2. Finding and evaluating the evidence base
3. Proposing a research project or an evidence-based practice

In the previous chapter, we explained that the persuasiveness of your writing will depend on your *credibility*, your ability to engage readers' *caring* about the topic, and your *competence* in searching the research literature and synthesizing it. As a student you establish your credibility and competence by demonstrating the extent to which your knowledge of a health phenomenon, policy debate, or professional issue is broad, nuanced, and thorough. You develop this knowledge through careful attention to discovering the best research evidence, accurate data, or current practice guidelines. You represent that knowledge by your skill in synthesizing and integrating the research literature, and citing those sources in a way that is consistent and professional. And you engage your readers' caring about the topic by demonstrating the significance of the clinical phenomenon and its impact on patients.

Step 1: Identify a Clinical Problem for a Writing Assignment

In your nursing specialty courses, like maternal-child health, you may be asked to write papers on a clinical problem relevant to that specialty. How do you identify a clinical question or problem? Begin by considering areas of clinical practice that could be changed to improve patient care—for example, what have you observed in your obstetrical clinical rotation that is particularly of interest to you? Perhaps you took care of a new mother on the postpartum unit who seemed depressed. Postpartum depression is a good topic for a paper.

You need to narrow the topic of postpartum depression, however, before you start your writing assignment. There are three ways to narrow your topic.

Reviewing the Literature Will Help You Focus the Clinical Problem

Upon reviewing the literature, you might find that more focused problems on postpartum depression would be (1) screening for postpartum depression, (2) treatment approaches, (3) risk factors for postpartum depression, or (4) the impact of postpartum depression on mother–infant interaction. Cheryl Beck can share with you an example from her own clinical practice to illustrate this process:

> When I was a junior faculty member at a university, I taught both the didactic maternity nursing course and also the clinical component. I had students in labor and delivery, postpartum, and the nursery. During my clinical groups' maternity rotations, I observed what appeared to be a distorted sense of time in women during the birthing process. For instance, one time I had a nursing student assigned to a mother who had just had a cesarean birth. The mother requested some pain medication, so the student and I went to get it for her. We were gone for no more than 10 minutes. When we walked into the mother's room with the medication, she started yelling at us saying: "You know how much pain I was in; why did you take over a half hour to come back!"
>
> On a different day one of my other nursing students was assigned to a woman in active labor. The patient requested some pain medication; so we went and got it. As we entered the room the woman was apologizing to her husband saying, "I'm sorry. I know I had promised I would have a natural childbirth but I have been pushing for over an hour and I can't do it anymore without some pain medication." Her husband looked at us as we stood in the doorway with

a look that seemed to say: What in the world is wrong with my wife? In reality his wife had only been pushing for no more than 15 minutes.

After the student administered the pain medication to her patient, we stepped out of the labor room. My student then asked me, "Does that happen all the time with women in labor that their sense of time gets screwed up?" I told her that I had been noticing a pattern of distorted time in childbirth with some of my patients, but I did not know if any research had been conducted on this topic. I said, "Let's go and review the literature." What we found was that no research had been conducted on time perception during childbirth. Moreover, only a couple of studies had been conducted on time perception during the postoperative period of patients who had major surgery. This pattern of distorted

What If I Don't Have Access to a Clinical Practice?

Start by asking your nursing professors for suggestions about clinical or professional issues. Consulting with your professors, you should be able to brainstorm a short list of topics.

You could also pay attention to health issues in communities that you are a part of or health issues that have appeared recently in the news.

Professional librarians are also very helpful in guiding students toward topics for which there is sufficient literature.

Finally, let the research literature guide you by drawing on topics that are supported by recent research studies.

senses of time during labor and delivery became the topic of my doctoral dissertation research in 1983.

Cheryl later revised her dissertation in the form of a peer-reviewed journal article: Beck, C. T. (1983). Parturients' temporal experiences during the phases of labor. *Western Journal of Nursing Research, 5*, 283–295.

We want to emphasize that there is no clean formula for finding and narrowing a research topic. It is messy, circular, and in need of revision throughout. It involves a great deal of trial and error.

Using the Right Technical Terminology Will Help You Focus the Clinical Problem

After you have found a suitable topic, the next step is to develop a list of keywords and search terms, which you can use alone or in combination with each other to help you conduct further searches of the literature.

If your topic were postpartum depression, you might formulate one or more of the following research questions:

- What are the effects of postpartum depression on mother–infant bonding?
- In whom is postpartum depression most likely to occur, younger primiparous mothers or older multiparous mothers?
- What is the prevalence rate of postpartum depression in the first three months after birth?
- Why does postpartum depression occur?
- How might we screen for postpartum depression in a timely fashion?

Specifying a Type or Cause and a Specific Population Will Help You Focus the Clinical Problem

For example, pain is too broad a topic, so specifying postsurgical pain or osteoarthritis pain further narrows it. Further refinement occurs when you identify a specific patient population: adolescents with postsurgical pain or older adults with osteoarthritis pain. You could further narrow your topic by specifying the type of treatment that will be your focus: pharmaceutical treatment of adolescents' postsurgical pain or non-pharmaceutical complementary treatment of older adults' osteoarthritis pain.

Step 2: Formulate a Research Question

The basic questions that any nursing student should ask are as follows:

What?

What is the phenomenon I observe? What are its signs and symptoms? What are its empirical, observable, measurable aspects? In what ways does it differ from the norm or the ideal?

Who?

Who is affected by the phenomenon? Who is involved with it?

When?

When does the phenomenon occur in relation to other events? How frequently does it occur?

Where?

Where on the body does the phenomenon occur? Where in the health care system does it occur? Where in the community or in a geographic locale does it occur?

Why?

Why does this phenomenon occur? Why does it occur at some times but not at others? Why does it occur in some places or in some populations but not in others?

How?

How might we prevent the phenomenon? How might we more quickly identify or diagnose it? How might we treat or improve it?

Students often pose questions that are either too broad or can be simply answered by factual data. Here we show sequences of questions that exemplify a student's refinement of a research question.

Moving from broad and general to narrow and specific research questions:
1. *What is stigma?* (too broad)
2. *What is mental health stigma?* (narrower but still very general)
3. *What is the social stigma typically associated with obsessive-compulsive disorder?* (focused without being too narrowly focused)

Moving from factual questions to interpretive questions based on factual information:
1. *What is the incidence of type 2 diabetes in Hispanic women?* (a sufficiently narrow topic, but one simply answered by consulting epidemiological databases)
2. *Why is the incidence of type 2 diabetes more prevalent in Hispanic women than in non-Hispanic white women?* (a precisely defined topic whose answer requires arguing on behalf of an interpretation of the evidence)

Once you have narrowed the focus of your clinical paper on postpartum depression and formulated a research question,

Start Writing Early

Even as you are formulating your research and evaluating the evidence base, you should begin drafting. In this case, to get yourself started, you might ask the following questions:

- Why is the problem of postpartum depression so important?
- What are the concerns for the mother and her family?
- What is the prevalence of postpartum depression?

These key questions will help you focus the remainder of your research on the specific topic you identified and help you stay focused on the significance (the "so what?") of the topic.

for example, on the risk factors/predictors of this postpartum mood disorder, you are set to review the literature.

Step 3: Find the Evidence Base

When both of us were in our undergraduate and graduate degree programs, conducting literature searches for a term paper, a master's thesis, or a doctoral dissertation required us to navigate through different spaces of the library and visibly different formats of books and other print publications in order to find up-to-date information and journal articles. We began in what was called a reading room or a reference room, using handbooks, almanacs, and indexes. With these we identified other scholarly books or journal articles. Securing those books required us to go to other parts of the library: the stacks (for books) and the serials collection (for journals). Journals were visibly different from books and were printed in different sizes and formats. In other words, there were clear physical distinctions among the different kinds of sources of information.

Primary vs. Secondary Sources

At this point we want to make a distinction between primary sources and secondary sources. *Primary sources* are "first-hand reports of facts or findings; in research, the original report prepared by the investigator who conducted the study" (Polit & Beck, 2017, p. 740).

Secondary sources are "second-hand accounts of events or facts; in research, a description of a study prepared by someone other than the original researcher" (Polit & Beck, 2017, p. 744). When you read one author's summary and analysis of another author's research study, you are reading a secondary source.

While you might be tempted simply to trust and cite the secondary source, we urge you to look up the primary source and read it for yourself for three reasons:

- You want to grasp the literature yourself.
- You cannot always trust that the author citing a source has represented it accurately (i.e., the author may have been careless in reading or summarizing the article).
- You cannot always trust that the author citing a source has cited it correctly (i.e., the author may have made transcription errors). The principle of international diplomacy applies here: *Trust, but verify.*

We are telling you this story not to reminisce about how hard we had it "back in the day," but to make a point about how different (but also similar) your experience of conducting literature searches is compared to many of your professors' experiences. Today, your mobile phone, tablet, or laptop can deliver more health information than has ever been known before. Your search process is considerably less labor intensive than it was for us. But the ease of searching the Internet can be misleading. You cannot rely on a simple Internet search to yield good information.

Like us when we were students, you have to access the scholarly literature. There are nearly 400 U.S. or international nursing professional and research journals, not to mention even more biomedical and health science journals, so the sheer volume, even of reliable health research, leaves many students confused. Here we provide you some maps through this cluttered information landscape. See Table 2.1 on the next page.

Kinds of Sources

Three kinds of resources that you are most likely to use are:

- Background reference information
- Current statistical information databases
- Journal article indexes (chiefly the Cumulative Index to Nursing and Allied Health Literature and PubMed)

Background reference information

Reference works or reference databases, as the name implies, *refer* you to the research literature. They are not sources of original research. As a result, you generally do not use reference works as sources in your writing, and thus you do not cite them. Reference works include:

- Dictionaries
- Encyclopedias (including Wikipedia)
- Handbooks
- Textbooks

TABLE 2.1 Information Sources

	Types of Content	Why It Is Useful	How It Is Limited
Background reference information	Encyclopedias, handbooks, websites, and textbooks	Provide general information for the student studying a phenomenon	May be outdated, sources may not be reliable, not peer-reviewed, not primary sources
Statistical information databases	Demographic and epidemiologic data	Demonstrate prevalence, frequency, correlations, risk factors, populations affected	Do not fully represent the impact on individuals: "Statistics are human beings with the tears wiped away" (Selikoff, 1991, p. 126)
Online databases of journals	Peer-reviewed research literature; quantitative, qualitative, and mixed-methods studies; randomized controlled trials	Provide the strongest and most current clinical evidence	Each has typical study limitations (recruitment method, sample size, research design).

- Library subject guides
- Popular guide books (like beginners' or "Complete Idiots'" guides to subjects)

While these materials are often written and published by reliable and expert authors, they lack the precision and rigor of research publications. Although you likely will not cite a reference guide in your scholarship, you can still use them for two purposes:

- To make sure that you understand the general landscape of the topic
- To discover research sources (usually included in the bibliography or references section of a reference book or encyclopedia article)

A Word About the Internet

The reference guides, databases, books, and journals held by a library are carefully reviewed and approved by subject specialist librarians (often upon the recommendation of researchers and scholars in the discipline). In contrast, on the World Wide Web anyone can publish anything, no matter how inaccurate or downright false it might be. And the current technologies for web design make it possible for any website to look authoritative, accurate, or reliable, even when its information is not.

At the very least, you need to ask the following questions:

- *Who is the author of this material?* Anonymous web pages should raise a yellow caution flag.
- *What is the expertise of the named author?* Non-experts often feel at liberty to publicize their views and to publish pseudo-science. Generally, unless the expertise of a non-expert author is as a patient reporting on personal experiences but not making scientific assertions, you should not use the source.
- *What entity has published the material?* Self-published websites, websites published by unreliable entities with an ax to grind, or websites with an overriding profit motive should be scrutinized carefully. If there is no clear publishing entity, you should move on to a more reliable source.
- *How current is the material?* Web pages can languish for years without any revisions or corrections, and it is often difficult to determine when a web page was last edited. This information should appear somewhere on the page, usually at the bottom.

Statistical information databases

Governmental organizations are required by law to undertake accurate data collection and to make it publicly available. Nongovernmental organizations carefully ensure their credibility by providing reliable and accurate information. As a result, factual questions may be answered using statistical databases.

Among the more reliable statistical information databases are:

- U.S. Centers for Disease Control and Prevention
- National Institutes of Health
- U.S. Census Bureau
- State public health departments
- Disease prevention and treatment advocacy organizations (e.g., American Cancer Society, American Diabetes Association, American Heart Association)
- Health professions advocacy organizations (e.g., American Nurses Association, American Medical Association)

Such databases are useful to answer questions such as: *What are the incidence and prevalence rates of type II diabetes? How many Hispanic people live in the United States or in your state? What percentage of the American population is obese or morbidly obese? What are the current guidelines for safer sex practices to reduce the risk of HIV infection? What are the standard treatments for heart failure?*

Journal article indexes

The gold standard for health research is the *peer-reviewed journal article* (including original research articles, integrative literature reviews, and meta-analyses and meta-syntheses). Peer-reviewed journals are the place where new research findings are published, usually on a monthly basis.

What Is Peer Review?

In the academic and research worlds, research articles undergo careful scrutiny before they are accepted for publication.

First, upon a manuscript's submission, the editor or assistant editors or an editorial board conducts a preliminary review, usually to determine if the manuscript is generally suitable for that journal.

If the manuscript passes that first stage of review, the editor will ensure that the manuscript has no information identifying the author before sending it on to two or three (or sometimes more) peer reviewers who are expert in the particular topic of the manuscript. The reviewers will not know who the author is; later, the author will not know who the reviewers are. (This is often called *double-blind* review.)

Then, the anonymous reviewers each will make a judgment about the manuscript: (1) it is ready for acceptance and publication in its present form (which rarely happens), or (2) it needs minor corrections before it can be published or significant revisions, after which it should be resubmitted for a second review (either of which commonly happens), or (3) it is not suitable for the journal (which can mean simply that it is the wrong topic for the journal or that it is poorly written).

Finally, once a peer-reviewed manuscript has been accepted for publication, it is copy edited by the journal and set in galley proofs for the author's review.

Publication usually occurs in two moments: first, digital online publication (sometimes called *epub ahead of print*), then later print publication (if the journal has a material print existence).

We need to caution you, however, that not every article in a scholarly, research, or professional journal is peer reviewed. Some articles have only been reviewed by the editor or editors, including editorials, personal essays, and summaries of the state of research.

We also need to caution you that not all journals are created equal. Some are more prestigious than others (and typically the higher the prestige, the lower the manuscript acceptance rate). Some are "niche" journals that focus on a particular phenomenon or a particular specialization. And some journals are money-making scams that collect from authors publishing fees (which can range from $500 to $2,000) and publish the articles with little or no peer review. These publishers may claim that articles undergo peer review prior to publication, but there is little evidence for this claim.

How do you know the quality of a journal? We often consult the website maintained by librarian Jeffrey Beall—http://scholarlyoa.com/—who keeps a running list of "Potential, Possible, or Probable Predatory Scholarly Open-Access Publishers." The International Academy of Nurse Editors (2014) has issued a statement to its members cautioning them about predatory open-access publishing. You do not want to use or cite articles from these journals or publishers, and you will want to avoid submitting manuscripts to them for publication.

Research Databases

There are two research databases that nursing students, nurse researchers, and nurses in clinical practice typically use: *Cumulative Index to Nursing and Allied Health Literature (CINAHL)* and *PubMed*. See Table 2.2.

TABLE 2.2   CINAHL and PubMed

	CINAHL	PubMed
Source	EBSCO Publishing, Inc.	U.S. National Library of Medicine, National Institutes of Health
Scope	Over 950 English-language nursing and allied health journals and publications. [Source: CINAHL Plus, n.d.]	4,500 journals published in the United States and more than 70 other countries. [Source: PubMed, n.d.]
Content	Although it indexes nearly a thousand journals, it only includes full text for more than 580 journals.	Typically provides the reference for articles but not direct access to the article content.

Because CINAHL is hosted and maintained by a for-profit company, EBSCO, you can only access it through a subscriber, typically academic libraries. By analogy, think of EBSCO as your satellite or cable TV provider, which does not produce its own programming but allows you to watch videos through its service.

The other major database, PubMed, is publicly available because it is maintained by the U.S. National Library of Medicine of the National Institutes of Health. Because PubMed is not a fee-for-service provider, it does not typically provide access to journals and their articles, only to the reference citation. Like EBSCO's CINAHL, PubMed is not a publisher; it is merely an index (a reference tool) that refers you to journals and their publishers.

When you use CINAHL or PubMed to search the literature, you will usually find an entry for each article that may include a detailed abstract that summarizes the article. **This database entry and its abstract are not the article!** Students sometimes mistakenly believe that this single-screen database entry is the article itself. For example, when searching for an

Appl Nurs Res. 2015 Feb;28(1):2-9. doi: 10.1016/j.
apnr.2014.04.004. Epub 2014 Apr 29.
Prenatal screening for intimate partner violence: a qualitative meta-synthesis.
LoGiudice JA.

Abstract

Aim:

The aim of this meta-synthesis was to glean an understanding of healthcare providers' experience with prenatal screening for intimate partner violence (IPV).

Background:

Prenatal screening guidelines for IPV are in place; however, a gap exists between these recommendations and
providers' practices.

Methods:

Noblit and Hare's (1988) approach to synthesizing qualitative research studies was utilized. Eight research reports were identified and produced a sample of 142
experienced women's healthcare providers from the
United States, New Zealand, and Sweden.

Results:

The synthesis revealed five overarching themes: (1) therapeutic relationship, (2) understanding what she is not
saying, (3) presence of partner, (4) variations of how and
when to discuss, and (5) "lost in the maze" of disclosure.
When analyzed as a whole, the five themes contribute to
a lack of universal screening for IPV.

Conclusions:

Given that IPV is a social problem with long-term negative sequela, providers are poised to identify women
during the perinatal timeframe to ensure adequate referrals and services to stop the cycle of violence.

Keywords:

Intimate partner violence; Meta-synthesis; Prenatal
screening; Women's healthcare providers

article by one of our students, Jenna LoGiudice, on partner
violence (2015):

That is not the entire article. What you see on the PubMed
database is a structured abstract—a one-page summary of the
article that has been divided into subsections. Using the
PubMed reference, you would next go to the CINAHL database to find Jenna's article in the journal *Applied Nursing
Research.*

Search Strategies

Whether you are using an index's established *subject headings*
or *keywords* of your own devising, the search terms that you
select, apply in combination, and add to will give you access to
the research treasure that you seek.

Subject headings

Subject headings are terms that have been devised by professional indexers (for example, at public institutions like the
Library of Congress and the National Library of Medicine, or
at private proprietary companies like EBSCO). Indexers apply

Mining Research Articles for Relevant Literature

There is a treasure to be found in research articles themselves. Another way of identifying articles related to the topic or phenomenon you've chosen is to examine the literature cited in research articles. Although this is not the most complete or systematic method (as a careful search of databases is), it is a helpful way of ensuring that you have discovered the most frequently cited sources. Of particular use are the literature review sections of a research article and the article's references. This technique is helpful after you have conducted your own search of the literature in databases because it helps you find sources your search may have missed, and it helps you see which sources are the most frequently cited touchstones.

these subject headings to books or journal articles that are included in a library's book catalog or periodical indexes. In order for you to retrieve the books or articles that you want, you need to know the precise subject headings. The U.S. National Library of Medicine has developed its own system, Medical Subject Headings (MeSH), which can be used in PubMed. You can learn more about MeSH terms at the NLM's website (1999, 2014).

Keywords

Keywords are terms that authors use to "tag" their articles. Keywords are also terms that you use when searching the literature. When authors submit an article to a journal, for example, they are required to supply keywords for indexing purposes. Those keywords are then entered into the database to allow other researchers to more easily find their article. However, not all authors are equally skilled in devising keywords, so in your search of the literature you may have to use trial-and-error methods with several different terms. Using several different approaches (and keeping track of the keywords that you have previously used) will yield more results.

You can use various search strategies to help you search keywords more effectively. For example, using the wildcard character of the asterisk (*) casts your net widely. For example, if you wanted to search for *nurse, nurses,* and *nursing,* type *nurs** into the search field. In addition, Boolean operators give mini-commands (e.g., *AND, OR, NOT*) that enable you to

What sparked Cheryl Beck's passion for researching and writing about postpartum depression came from her own clinical practice as a certified nurse-midwife. In the 1980s Cheryl saw first-hand how devastating postpartum depression was for new mothers. In order to provide better nursing care for her patients, Cheryl turned to the nursing and medical literature and textbooks to learn more about this debilitating mood disorder that strikes new mothers without warning. Much to her dismay, at that time only a few sentences about postpartum depression were included in any of the textbooks. She decided then to devote her research program to studying postpartum mood and anxiety disorders. Her research findings, however, had to be disseminated in order for Cheryl to help provide the "evidence" for evidence-based practice. Writing is essential in dissemination. Cheryl continues to write and publish articles and books on her research studies.

make complex searches of the indexes. For instance, if you wanted to find articles related to nurses and their secondary trauma or PTSD but not PTSD in veterans, your Boolean search might look like this: *nurs** **AND** *PTSD* **OR** *trauma* **NOT** *veterans*.

Step 4: Evaluate the Evidence Base

Find Gaps in the Evidence Base

Your search of the literature will reveal what we know about a clinical phenomenon. By carefully exploring and surveying the boundaries of what we know, we prepare the way for the discovery of new knowledge. Typically, gaps in the literature emerge from *Why?* or *How?* questions. We don't fully understand why a phenomenon occurs or how the mechanism of a remedy or therapy works. We know a treatment works, but we don't know the minimum effective dose. We don't fully understand how a disease process affects some populations differently from others. Typically, you will announce the gap in knowledge in your introduction to a paper.

Understanding Research Designs

Nurses can no longer rely on a bank of memorized information but instead must be skillful in assessing, evaluating, and applying new research evidence. Evidence-based nursing practice involves integrating the best research evidence with clinical expertise and patient preferences. Evidence-based practice involves a hierarchy of evidence from strongest to weakest to guide your clinical decision making. Nurses in clinical settings seeking the evidence base to inform their practice or nurse researchers committed to expanding the evidence base all employ quantitative methods, qualitative methods, and mixed methods (methods of both the life sciences and the social sciences). Whether you are preparing to enter the clinical practice of nursing or are preparing to become a nurse researcher, you need to understand the differences among these methods, their strengths, and their limitations.

By way of introduction to the three types of research methods, we provide Table 2.3.

TABLE 2.3   **The Three Main Research Designs**

	Definition	Data	Examples
Quantitative	Employ empirical statistical data to determine the relationships among variables and effects, in order to determine correlations or causality	Numerical, where statistical tests are used to compute *p* levels that indicate if the results are significant or not	*experimental* *quasi-experimental* *nonexperimental*
Qualitative	Employ surveys, interviews, and focus groups to understand populations' perceptions and feelings	Words rather than numerical data (e.g., themes, verbatim quotations from interviews or focus groups)	*phenomenology* *grounded theory* *ethnography* *narrative analysis*
Mixed Methods	"[R]esearch in which the investigator collects and analyzes data, integrates the findings, and draws inferences using both qualitative and quantitative approaches or methods in a single study or program of inquiry" (Tashakkori & Creswell, 2007, p. 4).	Both numerical and words	*convergent (concurrent) parallel design* *explanatory sequential design* *exploratory sequential design* *embedded design*

Quantitative research methods

Some nurse researchers use methods often associated with medical research, *quantitative studies* that employ empirical statistical data to determine the relationships among variables and effects, in order to determine correlations or causality. There are three major quantitative research designs: *experimental*, *quasi-experimental*, and *nonexperimental*.

- A true experimental design, often called a *randomized controlled trial* (RCT), is the most powerful of quantitative designs for testing cause-and-effect relationships. RCTs provide clinicians with the highest-quality evidence regarding the effects of an intervention.
- *Quasi-experimental designs* are weaker. This type of quantitative design also involves testing an intervention or treatment, but it lacks randomization, and sometimes it also lacks a control group. The major limitation of quasi-experimental designs is that causal influences cannot be as confidently determined as in experimental designs. Alternative explanations for the outcomes other than the intervention abound.
- *Nonexperimental designs* are studies in which the researcher does not intervene by controlling the intervention (the independent variable). Nonexperimental studies do not yield strong evidence for making cause-and-effect inferences. However, when evaluating quantitative evidence we need to remember that correlation does not demonstrate causation.

Qualitative research methods

Qualitative research is inductive, deriving its conclusions only after the researcher has collected, analyzed, and confirmed the data with participants, and its process can be described as flexible and emergent. Where quantitative research attempts to reduce a phenomenon to its smallest observable unit (e.g., lab measurements of blood cortisol as a marker of physiological stress), qualitative research attempts to open wide its arms and embrace the whole phenomenon (e.g., what physiological stress means to a patient, or how patients cope with physiological stress).

Qualitative research provides the nurse researcher with a privileged insider's view into the world of patients. Results from qualitative research are powerful, and qualitative findings allow nurses to walk a mile in the shoes of these patients. By understanding from the patients' perspectives what it is like to experience a specific physical or mental illness, we as nurses can better design effective interventions to help improve patients' outcomes and improve the quality of their lives.

- *Phenomenology* is a qualitative approach used to describe and understand the subjective meaning of human experiences. Nurse scientists using this method are looking to discover the essence of a phenomenon—that is, what makes a phenomenon or experience what it is.

Qualitative Research Can Help to Bring Visibility to Invisible Phenomena

In her 2015 qualitative study of caregiving for a loved one with dementia at the end of life, one of our students discovered that her research participants sometimes expressed a yearning for escape, with one of them saying, "'I just want Dad to be at peace. I can see fear in his eyes. And I just want it to be over for him. Watching him go through this is killing me. This was the first time that I so strongly wanted my Dad to leave this world'" (Lewis, 2015, p. 492).

- *Grounded theory*'s goals are (1) to discover the basic social psychological problem/central concern in a substantive topic/area, such as postpartum depression, and (2) to identify the process used to resolve this central concern or problem. This research design is called *grounded theory* because the researcher eventually generates a theory that is grounded in the data (rather than starting with a theory that guides data collection and analysis).
- *Ethnography* is a qualitative research approach that focuses on description and interpretation of cultural patterns, behaviors, and experiences. Nurse scientists using this approach are interested in investigating research questions such as *What are the patterns of behavior of persons in a particular culture regarding health and illness?*
- In *narrative analysis*, the qualitative nurse researcher focuses on story as the object of the investigation. Narratives help us to understand how persons make sense of the events in their lives. Narrative analysis looks for common patterns or structures in the narratives of research participants.

Mixed methods

Mixed-methods research is defined as "research in which the investigator collects and analyzes data, integrates the findings, and draws inferences using both qualitative and quantitative approaches or methods in a single study or program of inquiry" (Tashakkori & Creswell, 2007, p. 4). The major types of mixed methods designs include *convergent (concurrent) parallel design, explanatory sequential design, exploratory sequential design,* and *embedded design* (Creswell & Plano Cark, 2011).

- In a *convergent parallel design* the researcher concurrently collects and analyzes the data for both the quantitative and qualitative strands and then mixes the findings during the interpretation phase.

- When using an *explanatory sequential design*, the researcher first collects and analyzes the quantitative data, followed by collecting and analyzing qualitative data to help explain the quantitative results.

- In the *exploratory sequential design*, the researcher first collects and analyzes the qualitative data, followed by collecting and analyzing the quantitative data to help test or generalize the qualitative results.

- Lastly, in the *embedded design*, the researcher does collection and analysis for both the quantitative and qualitative data within a quantitative or qualitative design. A popular example of an embedded design is the use of a small qualitative strand within a quantitative experimental study to assess the process of the intervention.

What Kind of Research Is Best?

In nursing, our patients and their health issues are so complex that we need both qualitative and quantitative research to understand the whole of human experience. These two types of research complement each other. As Patton (1990) has observed, "Qualitative data can put flesh on the bones of quantitative results, bringing the results to life through in-depth case elaboration" (p. 123).

Another example from Cheryl's research illustrates this point. In 1995 she conducted a meta-analysis of quantitative research studies on the effects of postpartum depression on maternal–infant interaction. When combining the findings from the studies, she found that postpartum depression had a significantly large negative effect on mother–infant interaction during the first year after delivery (Beck, 1995). The results from this meta-analysis, however, were just numbers. What was the mothers' side of this story? What was the meaning of postpartum depressed mothers' experiences interacting with their infants and older children? In order to put the flesh on the bones of her meta-analysis, Cheryl conducted a qualitative study with mothers suffering from this devastating mood disorder (Beck, 1996). The following quote, which is from the first mother whom she interviewed for her study, illustrates the flesh that qualitative research can bring to complement and enrich quantitative findings:

> "My husband and son got back from the store. I think my 3-year-old son wanted to tell me about something that had happened. It was physically so hard to listen that I really remember just trying to put up some kind of wall so that I wouldn't be battered to death. At this point I was really sitting on the couch trying to figure out whether I could ever move again, and I started to cry. My son starting hitting me with his fists, and he said, 'Where are you, Mom?' It was really painful because I didn't have a clue as to where I was either. He was really trying to wake something up, but it was just too far gone. There was no way that I could retrieve the mom that he remembered and hoped he would find, let alone the mother I wanted to be for my new baby." (Beck, 1996, p. 98)

Evaluating the Evidence

Now that you have a better sense of the kinds of research literature you might find, you have to situate where the evidence falls on a hierarchy of studies for evidence-based practice. One common way of showing the relationships among different evidence strengths is a pyramid figure, which we have adapted here from Polit and Beck (2014) in Figure 2.1. The strongest evidence, at the top of the pyramid, comes from systematic reviews of multiple RCTs. These are the strongest because the evidence comes from careful syntheses of multiple studies. The weakest evidence is located at the base of the pyramid: expert opinion and case reports. These are the weakest because they represent merely anecdotal views that may be influenced by bias or isolated cases.

Keep in mind that within any one level in the evidence hierarchy, the quality of evidence can vary widely depending on how well designed the research study is. So even though systematic reviews of multiple RCTs are the gold standard for evidence-based practice, a poorly conducted review may have little value to you as a student, researcher, or clinical nurse. For the nursing profession, *best evidence* refers to study results that are "methodologically appropriate, rigorous, and clinically relevant for answering pressing questions—questions not only about the efficacy, safety, and cost effectiveness of nursing interventions, but also about the reliability of nursing assessment tests, the causes and consequences of health problems, and the meaning and nature of patients' experiences" (Polit & Beck, 2014, p. 24).

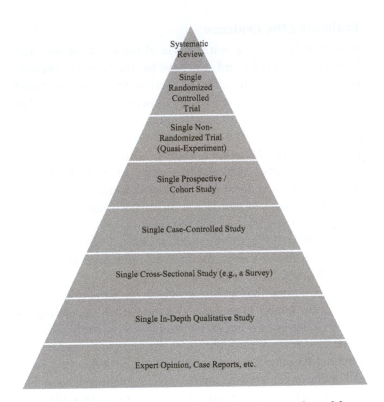

FIGURE 2.1 **Evidence hierarchy: levels of evidence. Adapted from Polit and Beck (2014, p. 23).**

Future chapters, such as Chapter 6, Literature Reviews, will help you move beyond analyzing and evaluating the literature to integrating it into various kinds of writing assignments.

CLINICAL REFLECTIVE WRITING

Throughout their courses, and even into a professional career, nursing students and nurses will write about their personal clinical experiences. In fact, although much of your academic career has required you to spend time preparing for quizzes, tests, and exams that assess your empirical knowledge about nursing (eventually leading to your taking the National Council of State Boards of Nursing Licensure Exam [NCLEX-RN®] for certification), one difference between a good nurse and a great nurse is the depth of your personal reflection about your clinical encounters with patients.

What Is Reflective Writing?

Reflective writing encourages you to focus on your analysis and evaluation of the clinical experience as well as consider what, if anything, you would do differently. Pre-licensure students, for example, may keep journals and diaries or write papers that require them to narrate significant clinical encounters or to reflect on clinical dilemmas in nursing.

The challenge in personal reflective writing is digging deep into yourself in order to unearth relevant details and their meaning. You may have a solid background in science that is shaped by empirical knowledge, which is invested in facts and evidence about patients' cases. However, personal reflection and reflective writing are learned behaviors. For example, Epp's (2008) literature review of reflective journaling in undergraduate nursing education reported that learning to write reflectively was a learned skill and having to create written documentation with a critically reflective eye on their practice is often difficult for students. According to this review, critical reflection took time to develop with feedback from faculty. Students' self-disclosure in their reflective writing increased as trust between nursing students and faculty increased. Epp also found in the studies reviewed that undergraduate nursing students initially tended to write primarily at lower levels of reflection. Fortunately, by using reflective writing, nursing students' perceptions of writing changed from the notion that writing was only useful to represent what they had learned to the understanding that writing was learning itself.

To give you a sense of the difference between superficial and deeper reflection, let's look at two examples.

Example 1: Superficial Reflection

Today I gave postpartum care to a 13-year-old girl who had just given birth to a 6 lb 3 oz baby boy. My young patient had a vaginal birth after a 14-hour labor. The one support person she had with her throughout labor was her older sister. The father of the baby was nowhere to be found. My nursing care consisted of checking her fundus to make sure it was firm, and to estimate the amount of bleeding every 15 minutes to make sure she did not experience postpartum hemorrhage.

In this example, while the nursing student shows competence in using technical terminology, she has not reflected on her feelings regarding caring for this very young mother who was still a child herself or reflecting on what she had learned. What an opportunity she missed!

Example 2: Somewhat Deeper Reflection

I just couldn't believe that a 13-year-old had just had a baby! I am 7 years older than my patient but I don't feel anywhere near old enough or mature enough to have a baby. I have all these goals in my life I want to achieve. How is this 13-year-old girl going to achieve any of her goals she had been dreaming of for herself now that she has a baby to take care of? To make matters worse for her it doesn't seem like there is any father around to help her raise this baby.

In this second example, the nursing student saw a connection between herself and her patient. Her *care* is obvious. Building off this sense of care for her patient, she might be better equipped to deliver competent, credible care to future patients because she sees their needs as human beings.

A still more sophisticated reflection might make connections not just between professional experiences and personal ones but also between those experiences and the content of lectures or readings covered. It might explore context (Would this same thing happen in hospitals in either poorer or richer

- *Credibility:* Have you provided sufficient detail in your narration of the clinical event?
- *Care:* Have you represented your own feelings about the clinical event and afterward?
- *Competence:* Have you analyzed your own experience and perceptions, deriving insights about yourself that you share with the reader?

neighborhoods? Have these issues changed over time? How does what you are seeing jibe with current social issues and movements?). It could also dig down to root causes (for example, rather than just lament that the father is not around, explore some of the social and economic reasons why that might be so).

Getting Started

There are a number of reflective models that can be used as guidelines for reflective writing. A popular one is Gibbs's (1998) reflective cycle, which entails the following:

- Description: What happened?
- Feelings: What were you thinking and feeling?
- Evaluation: What was positive or negative about the experience?
- Analysis: What sense can you make of the experience?
- Conclusion: What else could you have done?
- Action plan: If it happened again, what would you do?

Baker's (1996) four-step model offers nursing students another model:

1. Identify a clinical experience that you perceive as significant.
2. Describe in detail your thoughts and feelings and the events of that experience.
3. Address the significance the experience has for you, the personal meaning you derive from it.
4. Look at the implications of the experience, how it has affected or changed you.

We suggest the following process for writing a clinical reflection paper. As a nursing student the first level of reflective writing you will perform is the easiest: describing the clinical experience on which you have chosen to focus. You are reporting the events that happened, who was present, what you did, and the results.

Next comes a higher level of reflective writing where you assess, analyze, and evaluate your nursing actions. What was your rationale for your actions? What went well? What didn't go so well? What would you do differently next time if you were in the same situation with a patient? Which of your nursing actions would you keep the same? Take time to reflect on the nursing care you gave a patient.

Next, move beyond the individual case. Reflect on your future actions and role as you continue in your nursing program caring for more complex patients. *Has this patient interaction you just reflected on in your journal helped you to identify and manage your patients' needs better in the future? What plans do you have to expand your knowledge of the evidence base and skills you felt were deficient?* You could write something like:

- "This clinical experience with my patient has motivated me to . . ."
- "I need to improve on . . ."
- "I feel more confident now if I am assigned another patient with a similar nursing diagnosis because . . ."

As you write reflectively at a higher level, not only will you describe events about your nursing care, but you will also include more discussion of what happened and will explain the rationale behind your nursing actions. *What alternatives could there have been to the care you chose to give your patient? What might your actions in the future look like? Have you developed new and different perspectives on that clinical situation to guide your future actions?* You now can write about your awareness of what influenced your nursing care.

Don't forget that we learn from our clinical mistakes or disappointments; acknowledging them demonstrates maturity and confidence. *If you have not achieved the goals you had set for your nursing care that day, what prevented it? What could you have done differently to achieve your goals?*

Evaluating Reflective Writing

You may think it impossible for your professor to grade your reflective writing, but faculty have developed a number of ways to assess your writing while also acknowledging the personal nature of your work. Nursing faculty will offer specific prompts for the kinds of information and reflection that they are seeking in this assignment. You want to make sure that you are showing them the kinds of observation and reflection they seek.

One of our colleagues, Assistant Clinical Professor Helen Zakewicz, uses a formal structured design for clinical reflection assignments, which you can see here from one of her students. See Figure 3.1. The first section invites the student to think intentionally before the clinical encounter. In the next section of this structured reflection, the student addresses both what she did and how she felt about and learned from what she did.

Another of our colleagues, Dr. Desiree Diaz, gives her students more open-ended and less formal reflective assignments in an innovative nontraditional clinical setting combined with service learning, community engagement, and clinical simulation. See Figure 3.2 on page 57. One of her students provided us with the following example of her reflective writing.

Depending on the extent of your knowledge and clinical experience, as well as your stage in life, you bring to clinical reflection writing different perceptions and insights. The most important skills in this assignment are the ability to observe and report in concrete detail and the capacity for personal reflection and insight about the significance of what you saw and did in the clinical encounter.

Name: Meagan	Date: November 13, 2014	
Clinical site: Student Health Services	Nurse (first name): Priscilla	
3 objectives (complete before clinical)	Were objectives met? Why?	
1. Become comfortable in my new clinical setting.	Yes. At first I was uncomfortable just because I have been going to the hospital for so long and was so used to its procedures and the steps on how to do things. I was put into a different setting so of course I had to find my bearings. It was very good though. In one day I learned a LOT. We went over the steps the nurses do when they see the student (patient) for the first time. A staff nurse was very helpful and explained everything she was doing clearly.	*Here the student is expected to think ahead of the clinical encounter with a goal-directed rather than random approach to the clinical encounter.*
2. See new and different things.	Yes. We had a variety of cases! We observed a doctor put in stitches, wound care, a sebaceous cyst get removed, and an acute case where a male patient was very sick. Every case presented things I have never seen which was wonderful and Priscilla was very helpful in explaining everything she was doing.	
3. Learn something new.	I know this objective is very vague, but I wasn't sure what I was going to experience while I was at SHC. But, I learned a lot!!! Like I said previously, I saw many new things. With every patient, I learned something new. I was able to watch the doctor put in three stitches just above a student's eyebrow, I saw her take out a sebaceous cyst (where she packed the wound after so the healing is happening from inside out), and I saw a wound change/debridement. Furthermore, the staff nurse took another student and me aside a lot and we practiced on each other. We went through the head to toe assessment, which I found very helpful.	

FIGURE 3.1 Excerpt of a student's structured clinical reflective writing.

Skills you used:	Nursing interventions you saw/used:	Brief lists are acceptable here.
Basic assessment Head-to-toe assessment Use of an otoscope Assessing vitals Therapeutic communication Clinical thinking skills	Therapeutic communication Ongoing assessment Collaborative intervention with doctor, x-ray technician	
How did this experience make you feel? I felt like I learned a lot! I loved seeing the diverse cases that were brought to me and I loved how they all gave me different experiences. I know I learned a lot more than I listed to the right, but it's so hard to pinpoint everything that you learned in a jam-packed day! I was nervous in the beginning just because I was not oriented to the Student Health Services, but after an hour I felt calm and oriented and ready to learn more and more and more.	**What did you learn?** • You always want the wound to be smooth on the edges when it heals (so it heals evenly and not bumpy) • SHC protocol (their ABCDs) • Head-to-toe assessment (knew this already, but it was a nice review) • Ways to handle uncomfortable situations in terms of communication • How to screen for flu • Where you want to place stitches when giving stitches/putting them in (or where doctors like to place them) • The importance of receiving history (I knew this but it was emphasized today) • What a dislocated bone might look like on an x-ray (literally out of place and out of line) • How to put on a splint	*The student identifies both personal perceptions and more concretely what was learned.*

FIGURE 3.1 *(Continued)*

This was my first week at soccer camp and I must say I was pleasantly surprised at how it turned out as a clinical placement. I had expected to have much more down time than actually occurred, and while a part of me is stressed that I was not able to study as much as I had planned, I am also very pleased at the fact that I got to experience some medical events while I was there.

My first day was pretty slow in regards to medical events that happened. On another field, however, a 13 year-old boy had an acute asthma attack that manifested as chest and shoulder pain. He had no history of asthma, and was sent to the hospital upon which they conducted a chest x-ray and 3 nebulizer treatments. He was diagnosed with exercise-induced asthma and was given an inhaler with a spacer to use from now on. While I was disappointed that I was not able to be at the field where this occurred, I was also proud of myself because when the other student I was with told me the details of the situation, my first thought was that it was probably asthma, regardless of the fact that I was not yet aware of the diagnosis. It made me feel confident that I was able to use the information given and the knowledge base that I had to formulate a diagnosis in my mind prior to hearing the actual medical diagnosis assigned to that particular person.

On my second day I was able to participate in a case of a head injury of a 15 year-old boy. He had jumped up to attempt to hit the ball with his head while at the same time another player had attempted to kick the ball. The 15 year-old was kicked in the head during the process and was brought over to us in order to have an evaluation done. The first steps we took were to assess his vital signs, get a pain rating with a location and quality, and to ask if he had any dizziness or blurry vision. We had him rate his dizziness, blurry vision, and pain on a scale of 1-10 and then I had the opportunity to assess his pupillary reaction to light. His pupils were equal and reactive to light, but he was in fact dizzy and had a headache that increased when he stood up and walked. We also obtained a brief history on him by asking him if this has ever occurred before, and when. I also was able to witness a balance test conducted on him once we returned to the lounge area, which I had not known was part of a concussion assessment.

Having the opportunity to be out in the field with the players and conducting my own assessments has already instilled more confidence in me than I had coming into this clinical. It is a completely different type of learning experience to go from reading about clinical manifestations of an event, to actually witnessing and assessing those symptoms in person. I am still hesitant sometimes in fear that I may make a mistake or be unsure of myself, but I am sure that is something that will come in time as I gain more experience in the field. Overall this week has been really informative and refreshing, and I have realized how different nursing is when dealing with kids. Again, this is something I am sure comes with time, but I am already feeling more confident in the way that I approach the kids and communicate with them about health topics. I am certainly excited to see what Sunday has in store for me, and to begin to get to know the next group of kids coming into camp this week.

FIGURE 3.2 **Excerpt of a student's unstructured clinical reflection.**

Aren't reflection papers just subjective?

In fact, several education researchers have identified levels of reflection to assess nursing students' reflective writing. Powell (1989) developed an instrument to assess reflectivity in nurses based on Mezirow's (1981) six levels of reflectivity:

1. Reflectivity: awareness, observation, description
2. Affective reflectivity: awareness of feelings (your own)
3. Discriminant reflectivity: assessment of a decision-making process, or evaluation of planning or carrying out of nursing care
4. Judgmental reflectivity: being aware of value judgments and the subjective nature of these
5. Conceptual reflectivity: assessment of whether further learning is required to assist in decision making
6. Theoretical reflectivity: awareness that routine or taken-for-granted practice may not be the complete answer, obvious learning from experience or change in perspective. (p. 827)

CLINICAL CASE STUDIES

If reflective writing is an informal way for you to deepen your understanding of your developing nursing practice, writing a formal case study enables you to share with a wider audience your experiences in a significant clinical encounter. In addition, when you publish a case study (as many undergraduate honors students and graduate students do), you add to the knowledge base that informs evidence-based practice.

Individual cases (i.e., a significant clinical encounter with one patient) can also provide you with important personal and ethical knowledge that confirms the empirical knowledge that you learn in lecture courses.

Credibility: Have you documented and synthesized your review of the literature concerning the clinical case?

Care: Have you demonstrated the clinical significance that this case represents?

Competence: Have you adhered to the ethical obligation of preserving the patient's confidentiality? Have you provided sufficient detail about the case?

What Is a Case Study?

The case study is a genre of clinical science writing, first developed in medicine and now used extensively in academic and professional nursing. While all nursing writing is clinical writing, the case study allows you to think more deeply about your interactions with patients, moving beyond applying skills, while also using and adding to the evidence base.

You might hear the term *case study* used to describe kinds of "case reports." Frawley and Finney-Brown (2013), for example, list the main types of case reports:

- Diagnostic or assessment reports
- Treatment or management reports
- Educational reports

In *diagnostic case reports* the writer focuses on how a rare or unusual case was identified. *Treatment reports* describe the patient care, treatment, management, and results of individual cases. In *educational reports* the writer addresses current practice strategies and literature reviews. We use the term *case study* broadly to include a variety of academic writing assignments, including a *clinical incident paper* and an *ethical case paper*.

Case studies or reports are written for various purposes—for example, to describe an unusual or rare disorder, to provide insight into a disease, to describe a challenging differential diagnosis, to detail a rare or novel adverse event of an intervention, to document a mistake in health care, or to advance a clinical hypothesis that is novel (Juyal, Thaledi, & Thawani, 2013).

The benefits of case reports are important. They facilitate learning from past experiences, allow clinicians to share management plans for challenging patients, and facilitate development of practice guidelines (Aitken & Marshall, 2007).

Starting to write a case study:

1. Identify a difficult or unusual case.
2. Conduct a thorough literature review concerning the clinical phenomenon.
3. Identify a gap in the evidence base.
4. Confirm that you are making a unique contribution.

They are also excellent ways for you to develop problem-solving skills.

Getting Started

Prior to starting to write a case study, you need to conduct a thorough review of the literature to determine what has already been published related to the topic of your case study (see Chapter 2 for advice on how to conduct a search of the literature). *Where is the gap in the evidence base that your case study can fill?* If your case study cannot make a new contribution to the evidence base, you should consider selecting a different topic.

Composing the Clinical Case

Common components of a clinical case report include:

- Title
- Introduction
- Description of the case
- Discussion
- Conclusions
- References

Novice writers typically make these common errors with case studies:

- Using outdated epidemiological and demographic statistics in the introduction. (Ideally you should use data from the past five years but no older than the past ten years.)
- Describing the case in generalities rather than specific details.
- Providing no comparison of their observations with the findings of previous literature. (The case study should show either that previous findings have been confirmed or contradicted, or something entirely new has been discovered.)
- Providing no synthesis that enables the reader to understand the implications for nursing practice. (You need to explain the "So what?")

Title

Whether you are writing a case study as a course assignment or for publication, you will want to give your paper a descriptive, concrete title. For example, *A Case Study of an Elderly Hispanic Male with Type 2 Diabetes and Multiple Comorbidities* is far more descriptive and clear than *A Diabetes Case Study*. The detailed title provides important demographic information about the patient as well as diagnostic information.

Introduction

In the introduction, you should clearly and concisely describe the purpose of the case report, as well as your rationale for writing it. Here you should also highlight the merit of the case study to engage the interest of the reader. Current statistics on the prevalence of the condition or situation that is the focus of the case study are perfect to present in the introduction. Moreover, in this first section you describe the results of a focused literature review that sets the stage for the case presentation.

For example, Cheryl Beck published a case study of an adult survivor of child sexual abuse and her labor and delivery and breastfeeding experiences (Beck, 2009). Cheryl wrote this case study to raise clinicians' awareness of the long-term, devastating impact that child sexual abuse can have on women during childbirth. In this case study Beck introduced the problem this way:

> One of the proposed targets of Healthy People 2010 is to have 75% of women breastfeeding in the early postpartum period, 50% at 6 months, and 25% at one year (U.S. Dept. of Health & Human Services, 2000). On a more global level, the World Health Organization (2002) recommends exclusive breastfeeding for 6 months. In our zeal to achieve these goals, clinicians need to be cognizant that for some women with a history of childhood sexual abuse, breastfeeding may be negatively affecting their mental health. They may struggle to continue to breastfeed under the weight of societal pressure to provide their infants with the well documented benefits of breast milk (Kendall-Tackett, 1998). Although there are varied extremes of the prevalence of child sexual abuse, evidence is mounting that suggests that at least 20% of adult women in North America experienced child sexual abuse (Finkelhor, 1994). In order to highlight some of the breastfeeding struggles women experience who have been sexually abused as a child, a case study is presented. (Beck, 2009, p. 92)

Description of the Case

In the next section, the case presentation, you describe the case in depth. This is the main portion of the case report, which can include all relevant information such as the patient's demographics, past medical history, family and social history, current medical problems, laboratory and diagnostic data, past medication history, assessment, and treatment (Cohen, 2006). Here are two excerpts from Cheryl's case study to illustrate how quotations from patients provide a powerful glimpse into one woman's experience, alerting clinicians to the magnitude of this problem. The first quote focuses on the patient's labor experience:

> A haze of hospital labor room, nakedness, vulnerability, pain. Silence, stretching, breathing, pain, terror and then I found myself 7 years old again, and sitting outside my parents' house in the car of a family acquaintance, being digitally raped. The flashback to the abuse that I had experienced 23 years ago was not new. I always knew it had happened. What was different this time was that I felt the emotional response to it. I had never felt that before. In the midst of transition of the birth of my first baby, I finally felt it all in one shocking moment: the anguish, the shame, the horror, the violation, the massive breach of trust, the grief, the betrayal, the confusion, the despair and the dirtiness. (Beck, 2009, p. 94)

And the second excerpt focuses on the patient's breastfeeding experience:

> Of course I couldn't tell anyone what was really going on in my head when I tried to breastfeed. When I placed

my baby to the breast, I experienced panic attacks, spaced out and dissociated. It triggered flashbacks of the abuse and a sick feeling in my stomach. I hated the physical feeling of breastfeeding. I hated having to offer my body to my child, who felt like a stranger. Whenever I put her to the breast, I wanted to scream and vomit at the same time. My body recoiled at the thought of placing my baby to my breast. The thought of breastfeeding, which was sustaining my baby, was forcing me to relive the abuse. (p. 95)

However, keep in mind that patient confidentiality is both an ethical and legal obligation for nursing students and nurses, regulated by federal law in the Health Insurance Portability and Accountability Act (HIPAA) of 1996. Therefore, maintaining the patient's anonymity and confidentiality is key. Do not get so detailed in describing aspects of the patient that confidentiality could be breached. Accordingly, some of the demographic characteristics of the patient may need to be disguised (Bennett, 2011). For example, in order to protect the mother who was the focus of the case study on the adult survivor of childhood sexual abuse and its impact on her breastfeeding experience, Cheryl changed some of the patient's demographic characteristics.

Patient Privacy

HIPAA regulations regarding patients and research participants are very detailed. For further information visit the U.S. Department of Health and Human Services website: http://www.hhs.gov/ocr/privacy/index.html.

IRB Approval?

If possible, you might secure the consent of the patient described in the case study (or the patient's family) before publishing it. But does submitting a case study for publication require institutional review board (IRB) approval? Generally IRB approval is not required if the case study is descriptive rather than analytical and if the patient is not a participant in a research study. Case reports are considered educational activities that are not defined as *human subjects research* by the U.S. Department of Health and Human Services. Nonetheless, you should always consult with your university's or hospital's IRB or with the editor of a journal prior to submitting a case study for publication in case local policies differ.

Discussion

The last sections of a case study are the discussion and conclusions, where you compare and contrast this particular case with previously published literature. Similarities and differences in the case presentation versus what already is known in the evidence base and in clinical practice are the focus of these sections. In the discussion section you address what the case adds to the current evidence base, as well as any limitations of the case report. A brief summary of the essential components of the case study and a conclusion should end the case study paper.

Conclusion

So what? The final section of a case study will answer that question. In the conclusion you will offer guidance for clinical practice (your own and that of others) and even make recommendations for future research (e.g., "There is scant evidence in the research literature, which suggests that this phenomenon needs further study"). You will need to be careful, however, not to make sweeping generalizations or even recommendations for evidence-based practice built on only one case report. Anecdotal reporting adds to the evidence base, but evidence-based practice relies on more than anecdotal reports.

References

Unlike a clinical reflection paper, which is personal in its focus (what *you* did, how *you* felt, what *you* learned), a case study views your clinical experience through the lens of the evidence base. Your references should reflect your diligence in determining what is the current knowledge concerning the patient's health condition (e.g., type 2 diabetes with comorbidities) and demographic characteristics (e.g., elderly Hispanic male). As with any use of research articles or clinical practice guidelines, your references should be reliable and current.

RESEARCH CRITIQUES

In the previous two chapters we showed you how to prepare and write two common forms of clinical writing that you are likely to encounter in your nursing courses: clinical reflective writing and the more formal clinical case study. In this chapter and the next we show you how to do formal academic writing that examines the research literature more systematically. In this chapter we explain the *research critique*, in which you systematically analyze and evaluate one research article to determine its value and relevance. In the next chapter we explain the *literature review*, in which you methodically analyze and evaluate several research studies in order to draw implications for evidence-based nursing practice or further research.

Credibility: Have you chosen a recently published research article?

Care: Have you demonstrated that the research article represents a clinically significant phenomenon?

Competence: Have you paid attention to the fourteen criteria outlined in Table 5.1?

What Is a Research Critique?

A research critique is a way to work methodically through a research article in order to evaluate a research study's methods, findings, and conclusions. The critique also demonstrates to your professor that you understand how to be a knowledgeable consumer of nursing research.

Getting Started

As a nurse in clinical practice you do more than skim research articles for their main points. Instead you critically analyze and evaluate articles to draw conclusions and implications for nursing practice.

What kind of article will you critique (quantitative, qualitative, or mixed methods), and which article will you select? In some cases, your professor will assign you one. In other cases, you may need to select your own article, for which you can use the search strategies in Chapter 2. If that's the case:

- Make sure it is a research article—not a research summary, review, or editorial—whose first author is a nurse.
- Select one that is no more than five years old and that has been published in a peer-reviewed journal.

Remember the bottom line of evaluating evidence of a research report for nursing practice: *Do the methods used yield findings that can be trusted and applied to other groups and settings?* In Table 5.1, we identify the fourteen major criteria for your critique of a research article, comparing and contrasting the unique features of quantitative and qualitative articles. Each of these criteria terms can serve as a section heading to structure your critique paper.

TABLE 5.1 Guide to a Critique of Evidence Quality in Quantitative and Qualitative Research

Section Headings of the Critique	Critiquing Questions		
	Quantitative & Qualitative	Quantitative Only	Qualitative Only
Title		Are key variables and the population identified?	Are key phenomena and the population identified?
Abstract	Are major components of the study succinctly summarized?		
Introduction	How well was the research problem identified? Was there an appropriate match between the research problem and method chosen? Did the researcher make a strong case for the need for the study?		

After these preliminary details, you next examine the foundations of the article you have chosen to critique, including its grasp of the literature, the theoretical framework, and the hypotheses or research questions.

Section Headings of the Critique	Quantitative & Qualitative	Quantitative Only	Qualitative Only
Review of Literature	Did the researcher identify databases searched and key terms? Were current primary sources cited? Does reporting of relevant studies follow logically? Did resources adequately summarize the state of science on the study topic?		

Theoretical/ Conceptual Framework		Was a theory or concept described that provided the framework for the study? Was the theoretical/conceptual framework woven throughout the study?	Were philosophical underpinnings identified that guided the method?
Hypotheses or Research Questions		Were hypotheses appropriately stated?	Were research questions clearly identified?

Next, you analyze and evaluate the article's research methods and data analysis.

Section Headings of the Critique	**Quantitative & Qualitative**	**Quantitative Only**	**Qualitative Only**
Research Design	Was there an appropriate match between the research purpose and design chosen?	What specific type of quantitative design was used? Did the design minimize threats to internal validity and external validity?	Was a specific research design identified or was the study a general descriptive qualitative study? Did the researcher provide evidence of reflexivity?
Population and Sample	Was the population of interest identified? Was the setting described where the study took place? Were sample criteria and characteristics adequately described? Were sample selection procedures appropriate?	Was a power analysis done to determine adequate sample size?	Did the researcher state that data saturation (when additional data collection provided no new information or ideas) was achieved?

(Continued)

TABLE 5.1 *(Continued)*

Section Headings of the Critique	Quantitative & Qualitative	Quantitative Only	Qualitative Only
Data Collection	Were data collection methods appropriate?	Were the instruments used to collect data on key variables appropriate and adequately described? Were key variables operationalized?	What types of methods were used to collect data? Interviews? Observation? Did the researcher provide the interview questions?
Measurement		Did the researcher assess the reliability and validity of instruments used, and were levels adequate?	What strategies were used to enhance the trustworthiness of the data?
Procedures	Was the research team adequately trained? Were approaches used to minimize bias in how data were collected?	Was the intervention adequately described? Did the researcher periodically check for intervention fidelity?	Were interviews recorded and transcribed? Was the appropriate interviewing approach used?
Data Analysis		Was the appropriate statistical test used for the level of measurements of key variables? Were Type I and Type II errors minimized?	Was the data analysis technique appropriate for the qualitative research design used? Did the data analysis technique suggest the possibility of bias?

Finally, you examine the article's findings and provide a summary assessment of its strengths and weaknesses.

Section Headings of the Critique	Quantitative & Qualitative	Quantitative Only	Qualitative Only
Findings	How well were the findings summarized?	Were statistical significance levels identified? Were tables used to illustrate findings? Was information presented about effect sizes and confidence intervals?	Are powerful quotes presented to bring the results alive? Are figures or tables included to highlight qualitative findings? Do themes adequately represent the meaning of participants' voices?
Summary Assessment	Are limitations of the study identified? Do findings contribute to evidence-based practices? Are suggestions for future research offered? Are findings compared with previous research?	Were results discussed in relation to the theoretical/ conceptual framework?	Do the results seem trustworthy?

Critiquing a Quantitative Research Article

As we explained in Chapter 2, quantitative research relies on systematically gathering data that can be translated into numerical values. These data can then be analyzed through a variety of statistical tests in order to find patterns. Quantitative research may involve determining the *prevalence* of a health issue (how widespread), the *incidence* of a health issue (the rate of new cases), disparities in different populations, relationships among causes and associations of a health issue, or health outcomes following treatments.

When assessing the scientific merit of quantitative research evidence, keep in mind two criteria: reliability and validity. *Reliability* refers to the extent to which the measurement of key variables is accurate and consistent. *Validity* looks at whether the instrument used to measure a key variable is actually measuring the concept it is supposed to be measuring. Another component of validity refers to the relationship between the *independent variables* (the intervention that is being studied) and *dependent variables* (changes in the health of the patients studied). *As a consumer of a research report, how confident can you be that an independent variable (the nursing intervention being tested) really caused the improvement in a dependent variable (the patients' outcomes)? Or did confounding variables, not controlled by the researcher, cause the desired effect?*

Critiquing a Qualitative Research Article

The critique of a qualitative study follows the same protocol as the critique of a quantitative study, with some adjustments for the nature of qualitative research. As you see in Table 5.2, one of the differences in critiquing a qualitative study in contrast to a quantitative study's measurement is a critique's section called *Enhancement of Trustworthiness*.

Trustworthiness is at the heart of your assessing the evidence of qualitative research and determining whether you should propose transferring the research findings into clinical practice with patients. In assessing trustworthiness you consider the following five criteria (Guba & Lincoln, 1994):

- *Credibility*: the believability of the data and the confidence that you have in the truth of the findings and the interpretations of data

- *Dependability*: the stability of the data over time and under different conditions and contexts
- *Confirmability*: objectivity, which is conceived of as an agreement between two or more individuals reviewing the findings of a qualitative study for accuracy, relevance, and meaning
- *Transferability*: the extent to which you can reasonably transfer the results of a qualitative study to other contexts, such as other groups or settings
- *Authenticity*: the extent to which the researchers fairly and truthfully described participants' experiences (e.g., the descriptions were vivid and showed a range of realities)

Because these concepts may seem somewhat abstract, Table 5.2 serves as a guide to a focused critique of the evidence quality in a qualitative research report.

TABLE 5.2 **Evaluating the Trustworthiness of a Qualitative Study**

Aspect of the Study	Critiquing Questions
Credibility	1. Did the researcher keep a reflexive journal?
	2. Did the researcher write up comprehensive field notes during data collection?
	3. Did the researcher become so involved with the participants that he or she lost perspective?
	4. Were the interviews audiotaped so that they could be transcribed verbatim?
	5. Was there a triangulation of methods—that is, using multiple measures or tools to collect data?
	6. Were rich excerpts from participants' interviews included in the findings to bring them alive for the readers?
	7. Did the researcher have some of the participants validate the findings?
	8. Did prolonged engagement during data collection occur?
	9. Did persistent observation during data collection occur?

(Continued)

TABLE 5.2   *(Continued)*

Aspect of the Study	Critiquing Questions
	10. Did the researcher look for negative instances of his or her categories or themes? 11. Did the researcher state that data were saturated? 12. What were the researcher's credentials and experience in qualitative research?
Dependability	1. Were the interviews audiotaped and transcribed verbatim? 2. Did the researcher provide in-depth description of how data were collected and analyzed? 3. Could another researcher clearly identify and follow the steps in the decision trail used by the investigator of the study?
Confirmability	1. Did any colleagues review the data and results to concur with the findings? 2. If appropriate, were any inter-coder checks performed? 3. Were member checks with participants in the study done to determine congruence with the results?
Transferability	1. Were the participants who made up the sample typical of the population studied?
	2. Did the researcher sufficiently describe the demographic characteristics of the sample so that readers can determine if the results can be applied to other groups or in other settings?
Authenticity	1. Did the researcher provide a rich description of the participants' experiences so that readers can understand their experience? 2. Did the researcher fairly present the participants' experiences to show a range of realities?

Critiquing a Mixed-Methods Article

Now that we have examined the critique of a quantitative article and a qualitative article, we turn to a critique of an article that combines both types of research, the mixed-methods article. Creswell and Plano Clark (2011) suggest using four main criteria when you evaluate a mixed-methods study. Their criteria apply to the procedures for the research approach that the researchers used in the study, not the topic of the study. First, look in the methods section of the article. See if both quantitative and qualitative data were collected to answer the research question or to test hypotheses. Second, examine the methods section in detail. See if rigorous methods were used in both the quantitative and qualitative strands. Third, check the results and discussion sections for evidence of mixing the data. Finally, check to see if mixed-methods terms were used in the article.

By way of illustration Sandelowski (2008) used the analogy of apple juice, orange juice, and a mixed fruit juice to explain how mixed-methods research authors organize the findings of their qualitative and quantitative strands. Your breakfast menu might include apple juice and orange juice that you drink separately but not mix together. Or you might mix orange juice and apple juice together to produce a new kind of fruit juice. This new juice can be made up of more apple than orange juice, or more orange than apple juice, or equally apple and orange juice. Similarly, in some mixed-methods studies the authors describe the quantitative and qualitative strands, but each retains its separate, essential characteristics. In contrast, a true mixed-methods report blends the qualitative and quantitative strands.

Moving from Critique to Generalizability and Transferability

In the case of quantitative studies, you need to assess how relevant a particular study and its findings may be to other populations or contexts beyond those of the original study. *Generalizability* is the extent to which one study of one population sample in one context might be applicable to another sample in another context. In the current environment of evidence-based practice, generalizability or applicability is of great importance. Both quantitative and qualitative researchers have developed unique ways of addressing generalization. However, because generalizations can never be universal, Polit and Beck (2010) caution you to be careful when applying generalizable evidence. Directly generalizing from research results to specific patients in specific situations is often problematic. A good starting point is finding evidence that has a great degree of potential generalizability, but the evidence needs to be evaluated within specific clinical expertise and individual patient preferences.

Advances in the integration of quantitative and qualitative evidence have important implications for enhancing generalization, which occurs in a meta-analysis or meta-synthesis. *Meta-analyses* examine numerous quantitative studies; *meta-syntheses* examine numerous qualitative studies. Meta-analysis involves statistically integrating findings from multiple quantitative studies that examined the same research question. By integrating findings from subjects of different demographic characteristics, settings, time frames, and situations, the researcher enhances generalized inferences. The deficiencies of specific studies can be addressed with the help of a meta-analysis. In contrast, a meta-synthesis achieves interpretive translations by integrating the results of a phenomenon from numerous qualitative studies. The potential for meta-analyses and meta-syntheses to contribute to generalizability and transferability depends on how well these integrations of evidence are executed.

How to Generalize Quantitative Studies to Other Populations

Students often struggle with the concept of generalizability. Moreover, they are not alone in this difficulty because many news reports in mass media tend to hastily or carelessly generalize a single health study to larger populations. In the case of quantitative studies, you need to assess how relevant a particular study and its findings may be to other populations or contexts. In quantitative research, generalizability is regarded as a major criterion for evaluating the quality of the evidence from a study. Generalizability is the degree to which the methods used in a research study justify inferring that the results are true for a broader group than just the study subjects. You infer that the results can be generalized from the study's limited sample to a larger population. (*Population* refers to the total group of individuals who have common defined characteristics and about whom the study's findings are relevant.) The aim in quantitative research is to select a representative sample of the population. Using probability (random) sampling is the best method to achieve a representative sample. In random sampling every member of the specified population has an equal chance to be included in the study. The term *external validity* refers to the extent to which quantitative study findings can be generalized to settings or samples other than the one studied. Common in quantitative studies, however, are small convenience, nonprobability samples of subjects, but this type of sampling, because it is not random and may not be representative, poses the strongest threat to generalizability.

How to Assess Transferability of Qualitative Studies to Populations

In the case of qualitative studies, you need to assess how relevant a particular study and its findings may be to other populations or contexts. *Transferability* is the extent to which qualitative results can be transferred to other settings or groups. As a knowledgeable consumer of research you need to assess the transferability of qualitative studies. As a nurse your job is to evaluate the degree to which a qualitative study's findings are applicable to new situations. As a user of nursing research you transfer the results to another setting, and you can make good judgments about the extent of similarity of study contexts only if the qualitative researchers provided you with in-depth, *thick description* (i.e., rich and thorough description of background context, the sample, and findings). Evidence of saturation of the data (i.e., the point in data collection when any new data yield redundant information) enhances the likelihood that transferability can occur. To achieve thick description researchers need to provide in-depth information about their participants, contexts, and time frames: when the data were collected and from whom they were collected (demographic characteristics of the sample such as their age, education, gender, race, and ethnicity).

Quantitative Critique of Generalizability

In some of her undergraduate nursing research courses, Cheryl Beck assigns students to critique a quantitative study regarding its generalizability. Here is her abstract of one study that she asked students to critique for generalizability:

Johnson (2014) conducted a quasi-experimental study testing a nursing intervention to increase resilience in abused pregnant women. She used convenience sampling to recruit the women, which means that the sample was not random and might not have been representative. Abused pregnant women volunteered to be in the control group, and 50 abused pregnant women volunteered to be in the experimental group for a power of .80. The two groups were similar on all the demographic variables except age. Women in the experimental group were significantly older than women in the control group. After completion of the nursing intervention, data analysis revealed that women in the experimental group had significantly higher resilience scores than women in the control group.

The Resilience Self-Report Inventory (RSRI) was used to measure level of resilience. The past alpha reliability of the RSRI was .65.

After methodically reading the research article, one student analyzed these data in a first draft of her critique of the generalizability of this study's findings:

Johnson's (2014) quantitative study found that her nursing intervention produced significant results in increasing the resilience scores of abused pregnant women in the experimental group compared to the control group. The total sample of 100 pregnant women yielded a power of .80. Since Johnson reported a significant difference in resilience scores in the experimental group compared with the control group, nurses who practice with prenatal women can use this intervention as evidence to apply with these abused pregnant patients.

After consultation with Cheryl, the student revised her first draft in which she had concluded that the findings could be generalized beyond her sample of 100 pregnant women. In the revised critique below, the student was more specific about the study's methodological weaknesses that limit its generalizability. The student correctly concluded now that the study has limited generalizability:

Johnson's (2014) quasi-experimental study has a number of threats to internal validity. Because randomization was lacking, the threat of selection bias is strong. Women in the experimental group were significantly older than women in the control group. This significant difference in age is a competing hypothesis for the reason why the experimental group had significantly higher resilience scores versus the intervention. Even though the study achieved a satisfactory power level of .80, the use of a convenience sample limits the generalizability of the results of this study. Another limitation of the study was the unacceptable level of internal consistency reliability of the instrument used to measure the key dependent variable of resiliency.

Qualitative Critique of Transferability

In an undergraduate nursing research course Cheryl asked her students to break up into small groups and critique the transferability of the following qualitative study. Here is an abstract of the study students were assigned to critique:

Handlon, Slade, and Sizemore (2014) conducted a grounded theory study with caregivers of loved ones with Alzheimer's dementia (AD). The purposive sample consisted of six wives who were caring for their husbands who had AD. The first author conducted in-depth audiotaped interviews with each of the wives. All the participants were White with at least a bachelor's degree education. Analysis of the data revealed four themes that described the essence of the experience of caring for a loved one with AD. Powerful quotes were used to bring to life each of the four themes.

In each small group one student was elected to record the group's critique. Below is one small group's first draft:

Handlon, Slade, and Sizemore's (2014) grounded theory study provides nurses with vivid, powerful insights into what it is like for caregivers to provide daily care for their loved ones with AD. The audiotaped interviews provided verbatim transcripts to help with credibility of the findings. The results described in 4 themes certainly will benefit nurses when applying this qualitative evidence to their clinical practice. The sample of 6 wives who cared for their husbands with AD is spot on and provides high transferability of the findings to others caring for AD loved ones.

After consulting with their professor, the students in the small group revised their first draft in which they had missed some key weaknesses of the study's methodology. In their first draft the students concluded that the study's results were transferable in the clinical setting. The nursing students did not notice that the researcher had used the wrong data analysis method for grounded theory, plus the students did not pick up on the fact that the sample was homogeneous regarding ethnicity, education, and marital status. With those points in mind, they revised their critique:

In Handlon, Slade, and Sizemore's (2014) research report they identified the qualitative research design they used was grounded theory. Their data analysis yielded 4 themes, which are not the appropriate outcome of a grounded theory study. Themes are appropriate for a phenomenological study. In a grounded theory study the nurse scientist should discover the basic social psychological problem of a population being studied and the process used to resolve or cope with the problem. The sample recruited is not conducive to transferability. A sample size of 6 participants is too small for a grounded theory study, which should have between 20–40 participants. All 6 of the participants in the Handlon et al.'s (2014) study were White, wives, and highly educated. This homogenous sample limits the transferability of the findings. For example, can the study's findings apply to other family members besides wives who care for loved ones with AD? What about caregivers of other ethnic groups or caregivers who do not have college degrees?

Another of Cheryl's students prepared a particularly thorough and balanced evaluation of the transferability of another qualitative research study:

Polit and Beck (2014) define transferability as, "The extent to which qualitative findings can be transferred to other settings" (p. 75). Transferability is usually a positive aspect to the results. If there is a wide range of ages or diversity of ethnic groups, the study's transferability increases, and the findings can be used by multiple groups instead of just one specific group. In the case of Buxton and Snethen's (2013) study, the ethnicity was relatively spread out and included 11 Caucasians, 10 African Americans, and five Latinos. As for age, the youngest participant was 27 years old and the oldest was 66 years old. Another variable that increased transferability was body mass index (BMI). The different BMI groups included 30–34.9, 35–39.9, and over 40. In each of these characteristics (ethnicity, age, BMI) there was no one group that dramatically outweighed another group.

All of these data are presented in Table 2, "Participant Demographics," of the results section. The ethnicity age, body mass index, education, marital status and household income (2007) are subgroups of characteristics that are included in the table. Buxton and Snethen (2013) made the table very easy to read and added percentages to show how certain groups had a greater relevance. A study that has high transferability requires a rich amount of descriptive information. This study has a relatively high degree of transferability, giving the study a more significant value to other researchers conducting interpretive phenomenological studies.

The researchers' themes of (a) perceptions of health and healthcare, (b) respect me as a person, (c) establishing a healthcare connection, and (d) assertiveness is necessary, seemed to accurately portray all the information gathered. This was seen through quotes that were relevant to the themes. Each theme had at least three quotes that were directly supportive. A table that displayed the themes with their subthemes was included to provide easy observation of how the subthemes connected with their themes.

The well-prepared and critically informed clinician will take the time to perform the intellectual work of carefully analyzing and evaluating research sources. The peer-reviewed research literature is not perfect. It is often superseded by subsequent studies, and you can only safely assert, "To the best of our knowledge at this time . . ." You and your colleagues in clinical practice or your colleagues on research teams at a university need to understand the strengths and limitations of methods and of published results. Moreover, at a time when almost anyone can have access to recent research findings (often without being able to understand their meaning, significance, or limitations), you will become the expert who has to explain and qualify for patients recent health news in the media and caution against hasty generalizations or jumping to conclusions. Although your patients may believe that any material posted on a website is legitimate, for informed users of health research, "I read it on the Internet" does not inspire confidence. Whether you are reviewing the literature in order to write a literature review, to propose evidence-based clinical practice guidelines, or to prepare a research study of your own, you will bring a balanced critique to your reading and writing.

LITERATURE REVIEWS

6

If nursing has a signature writing genre, it may be the integrative literature review, which identifies a nursing phenomenon, searches the published research literature, synthesizes what is known and identifies what is unknown, and discusses the implications for nursing practice. The terms *integrative review* and *systematic review* are often used interchangeably, but you should be aware of key differences. *Integrative reviews* discuss the results of studies within the confines of a specific question in the clinical setting; thus, integrative reviews can include different types of research and not just randomized controlled trials. *Systematic reviews* rigorously compare and evaluate often only randomized control trials; they not only report the results of the studies but also appraise how reliably the research was conducted (McGrath, 2012). For both kinds of reviews you can apply the analytical tools explained in the previous chapter for critiquing a single study, but now you will need to assess several studies. As you get deeper into your literature review, you'll also want to flip ahead to Chapter 10, Synthesizing and Citing Sources, which includes further advice for synthesizing multiple sources into a larger review or argument, as well as instructions on how to cite sources.

Credibility: Have you performed and documented
a methodical literature search and selection
process?

Care: Have you explained the significance of the
phenomenon?

Competence: Have you methodically analyzed
and systematically synthesized the research
literature?

Getting Started

Choose a Topic

Obviously this is where you will begin your review of the literature. Sometimes your nursing professor will assign the specific topic, but other times you will be given the choice of a
topic. If you are given the freedom to choose, first you need to
decide on a general topic, such as postpartum depression,
before narrowing your focus. See Chapter 2 for guidance on
how to develop a focus for your clinical topic.

Search Databases

Your general topic will lead you to searching databases to determine just what has been published. Ideally you will conduct
a cross-disciplinary search, meaning that you will review not
just nursing literature but also literature from other health sciences, such as psychology and medicine. Remember that this
is just a first pass at the literature—for this one, you're brows-
ing article titles and abstracts, trying to catch up on the conversation that other nursing researchers are currently having
on your general topic. Take note of the articles and keywords
that spark your interest—those might give you ideas on how to

narrow your topic. See the sections in Chapter 2 on "research databases" and "search strategies."

Narrow the General Topic

Once you review the results of your initial search of databases, you can now narrow your topic down to a more specific and manageable topic, which typically involves adding at least one additional key term:

> General topic: Postpartum depression
> Narrowed topic: Effects of postpartum depression on infant development

One way to test whether you've narrowed your topic enough is to see if you can phrase it as a question: *What are the effects of postpartum depression on infant development?* Your question need not pivot, as this one does, on a cause-and-effect relationship (How does *X* affect *Y*?), although this is common. For example, you could ask, *How have treatments for postpartum depression changed over time, and what are the most current conventional and alternative treatments?* Or, *What do studies tell us about how non-Western cultures have recognized and addressed postpartum depression?* Or any number of other narrowed (and interesting!) questions.

Decide on Inclusion Criteria

Your initial search of the databases should also guide you in determining criteria for which studies you will include in your literature review. You will need to limit the number of studies in your literature review to make it manageable. Some examples of questions you can ask: *Will you limit how far back in years will you go? Will you include both quantitative and qualitative studies? Will you include studies conducted by researchers in all health care disciplines?* For example, you might decide that your inclusion criteria will include (1) studies published in the last ten years, (2) both qualitative and quantitative studies, (3) studies conducted by researchers in all health care disciplines, and (4) studies on mother–infant development during the first twelve months after birth. As you can imagine this still casts a wide net, so depending on the number of research articles that you find, you might narrow the inclusion criteria further (e.g., while still focusing on mother-infant development during the first twelve months after birth, reviewing only the quantitative nursing research literature published in the past five years).

All researchers need to limit their studies (and make those limits clear to their readers); however, as you search the literature you might decide to adapt your inclusion criteria based on what you are finding—but if you do that, be sure to go back and apply the limits consistently to all you have already done.

Determine if Retrieved Literature Meets Inclusion Criteria

Now you will decide which studies you will concentrate on in your literature review. Scan the titles and abstracts of the articles pulled up in your searches. If they meet your inclusion criteria, then you will keep them. For example, if you find a study examining the impact of postpartum depression on the cognitive development of preschool children, you would exclude it from your literature review since the sample of children in the study is older than one year of age.

Critique and Summarize Quantitative and Qualitative Studies

Take all the quantitative studies that met your inclusion criteria, begin to critique each one, and write up a condensed summary. Apply the strategies we covered in Chapter 5.

Make Tables to Summarize the Research Studies

Assemble a table that summarizes the research articles you've selected. This will help you organize your thoughts and give your reader (your professor in a course, your colleagues in a health care setting, or readers of a journal if you publish your review) an overview of the data. You can use this template:

Author (Year)	Sample	Research Design	Data Collection Times	Results

FIGURE 6.1 Template for organizing research literature.

Create a Topic Outline

While there are variations among literature reviews, here are the common sections:

1. Introduction
   a. Rationale explaining the importance of the topic
   b. Its significance to nursing
2. Method (literature review strategies that you used)
   a. Databases searched
   b. Range of years in which studies were published
   c. Keywords you used to search the literature
3. Findings
   a. Overview of results of literature review search
      i. Predominance of quantitative or qualitative research
      ii. Explanation of how you are organizing the remainder of the literature review
   b. Main body of the literature review
      i. Description of quantitative research
      ii. Description of qualitative research
   c. Summary and conclusions

4. Discussion
   a. Implications for evidence-based nursing practice
   b. Suggestions for future nursing research

Write Your First Draft

Fill in each section of your outline with the notes and summaries you have already written from the quantitative and qualitative studies that met your inclusion criteria. Your literature review should end by identifying gaps in the literature. If you noted any contradictions or inconsistent results, explain them in your discussion section.

Here we provide an example from one nursing undergraduate, including her first and second drafts. In the first draft she described one study after another but failed to link or synthesize them. There was no organized approach to describing the results of her literature review. Notice also that there are format errors with the in-text parenthetical citations.

Vietnamese Women's Homebirth Experiences in Vietnam and in Hospital Births in the U.S. (Draft 1)

There has been little and no recent research done in Vietnamese women's homebirth experiences in Vietnam and hospital births in the US. However, research indicates that cultural familiarity, traditional beliefs and practices, language, and the preference of a female midwife are several themes that arise in successful interactions with homebirths (D'Avanzo, C., 1992). Vietnamese women who have immigrated to the US in hopes of a better life, usually left their motherland at a low median age, and, consequently, included a substantial number of women of childbearing age (Davis, R. E., 2001). Women who then had given birth in US hospitals may have experienced

← The writer is making some effort to provide an overview in her introduction, but she does not reveal the methods she used to conduct the review.

substantial differences in their health care experience, such as in communication, during labor, and in implementation of antepartum and postpartum cultural and traditional practices and beliefs.

Comparative research finds two constant themes emerging from women's narratives of their childbirth experience; 1) difficulty in communicating with the medical and nursing staff and, 2) the lack of understanding about what was to happen and why (Liamputtong, P., & Watson, L. F., 2006). These Southeast Asian women's narratives touched upon the benefits and perils of having a cesarean birth and vaginal birth during their stay at a hospital in Melbourne, AU, and moreover the difficulties in communication and understanding that emerged with the medical staff during the childbirth experience; such as feelings of powerlessness, fear, trauma, and lack of postpartum cultural sensitivity (Liamputtong, P., & Watson, L. F., 2006).

In 2008, Lin & Wang conducted interviews with Vietnamese, Turkish, and Indonesian women who had to be at least 23 weeks pregnant to less than one year postpartum and speak Taiwanese or Mandarin about knowledge of pregnancy, attitudes toward pregnancy, and experience of medical services during pregnancy. The women were asked to fill out a questionnaire which included the demographic inventory scale (DIS), knowledge of pregnancy scale (KPS), attitudes toward pregnancy scale (APS), experience of medical services scale (EMSS), and the prenatal examination behavior scale (PEBS). Results from the study indicated lowest scores on self-care among women as well as a lowly attitude toward health during pregnancy (Lin, M., & Wang, H., 2008). Women showed more patient satisfaction in an artificial medical environment rather than a systemic or real one.

The writer has located good sources and is dutifully summarizing them, but she does not really evaluate or *synthesize* them. It is not enough that all the studies are on the same topic—she should be explaining how the studies relate to one another.

Yelland et al (1998) conducted interviews of Vietnamese, Filipino, and Turkish women, who were recruited from the postnatal units of three maternity teaching hospitals in Melbourne, Australia, on their postnatal experience. Results were grouped in themes based on statements made by the women after being asked open-ended questions about their postnatal experience. Overall, results showed that they valued the behavior and attitudes of staff during routine care as some of the major factors that helped shaped their perceptions and attitudes of their postnatal experience (Yelland, J., Small, R., Lumley, J., Cotronei, V., Warren, R., & Rice, P. L., 1998).

In the second draft the nursing student improves her introduction by telling the reader that five studies were found on the topic, four of which are qualitative studies and one of which was quantitative; she also developed the summary of each study in more detail. Notice she has corrected mechanical errors, including citation format and capitalization of the proper names of instruments.

Vietnamese Women's Homebirth Experiences in Vietnam and in Hospital Births in the U.S. (Draft 2)

There has been little research—and none recently—conducted on Vietnamese women's homebirth experiences in Vietnam and in hospital births in the United States. Five studies (four qualitative, one quantitative) were selected and reviewed to support this study. In one study with Southeast Asian (SEA) women, network sampling was used to recruit the women, 15 of whom were Vietnamese, 3 Cambodian and 1 Hmong (Davis, 2001). All women were either refugees or immigrants, of whom eight of the women

The writer follows her first sentence, which announces the topic and a gap in the research, with a second sentence that reveals her method—that is, how many studies she reviewed and of what kind. In introductions, academic readers value *both* kinds of framing statements up front: topic and method.

had given birth to children in their native country while nine in the US (Davis, 2001). Phenomenology was the research method used in this study where the health beliefs and practices of the women were explored to help bring meaning behind their postpartum recovery (Davis, 2001). Results showed that the three themes, (1) prolonged bed rest, (2) regaining balance in the body, and (3) the affiliation of women, gave meaning to their childbirth experiences and prospective well-being in the community.

In another qualitative study, 30 Laotian, 30 Vietnamese and 31 Cambodian women were interviewed and asked about their views of vaginal and cesarean births (Liamputtong & Watson, 2006). Recruitment was done by purposive sampling, where the three bilingual interviewers of the study identified their fellow members of the Laotian, Cambodian, and Vietnamese communities as potential participants. Additional recruitment methods were used, such as snowball sampling and theoretical sampling, where no more recruiting is sought once little or no new data arise. The in-depth interviews lasted three to four hours long, where the interviewers explored the women's perceptions of having a caesarean birth versus a vaginal birth. Women who had both a vaginal birth and a cesarean were asked more questions regarding their perceptions and experience of cesarean birth. They were asked to describe their afterthoughts when first told about it, feelings about having had a cesarean section, and how they perceived it in comparison to having had a traditional vaginal birth. Using thematic analysis as the research method, Liamputtong and Watson (2006) found three main themes that arose in Cambodian, Laotian, and Vietnamese women's experiences with caesarean and vaginal births: (1) trust in medical authority, (2) personal and

cultural ideology of reproduction and moth-
erhood, and (3) passivity, powerlessness
and cultural alienation.

In a cross-sectional study, Lin and Wang
(2008) administered structured questionnaires to 112 Vietnamese, 15 Indonesian,
and 2 Turkish women. Five questionnaires
were used, which included the Prenatal Examination Behavior Scale (PEBS), Demographic Inventory Scale (DIS), Knowledge of
Pregnancy Scale (KPS), Attitudes Toward
Pregnancy Scale (APS), and the Experience
of Medical Services Scale (EMSS). The
women were recruited via convenience
sampling from community health centers
from an undisclosed province in Taiwan.
Inclusion criteria required the women to be
of at least 23 weeks pregnant to less than
one year postpartum and speak Taiwanese
or Mandarin. Results from the study indicated lowest scores on the Knowledge of
Pregnancy Scale (KPS) and Attitudes
Toward Pregnancy Scale (APS), where all
women lacked knowledge in the area of
self-care and had low attitudes toward
health during their pregnancy.

In another qualitative study, Yelland et al.
(1998) conducted interviews of 107 Vietnamese, 107 Filipino, and 104 Turkish women,
who were recruited from the postnatal units
of three maternity teaching hospitals in
Melbourne, Australia, on their postnatal
experience. Interviews were conducted at
home and in the woman's language of
choice. They were prompted by the open-
ended question, "Thinking back now, please
describe any things about your care in
hospital after birth that you think were
particularly helpful/unhelpful" (Yelland,
Small, Lumley, Cotronei, Warren, & Rice,
1998). Results showed that the women
(41.6%) who found advice, information and

The writer has added labels to each study to reveal its methodology ("In a qualitative study," "In a cross-sectional study"). She has also added information about sample sizes and detailed more of the specific findings. She has corrected errors in capitalization and citations.

demonstration of care given in an empathetic and friendly way particularly helpful were more apt to be more satisfied with their postnatal experience. However, 71% of the women were less than "very satisfied" with their postnatal care, wishing for more support or assistance with both baby care and individual preferences. Over half (55.1%) of the women were unsatisfied with the attitudes and lack of assistance of the staff, which discouraged women to communicate their care needs, such as rest and relaxation.

....

This second draft, while more developed than the first, still requires further work. The writer should consider:

- Placing the description of the quantitative study either at the end of the literature review or at the beginning. Currently it is sandwiched in the middle of two qualitative studies, which is less sensible than clustering similar studies together.
- Reviewing the options for organizing a literature review noted below.
- Citing (and discussing) more than one study per paragraph, at least occasionally. Less experienced writers typically stick to discussing one study per paragraph. More sophisticated reviewers frequently bring closely related studies (especially those with similar methods, or those with similar or contrasting findings on some common variable) into the direct conversation with one another—often in the same paragraph, or even in the same sentence. Notice how the "Literature Review for Fear of Childbirth in Women with a History of Sexual Abuse" later in this chapter does this frequently but the two examples immediately above do not.

- Ending the review with a brief summary and identification of a gap in the knowledge that calls for more of a specific kind of research.

Most literature reviews go through several rounds of revision, and each round should not be just about adding sources. Adding is fine, but revisiting your organization to make sure it is as logical as it can be is especially important.

Consider Common Patterns for Organizing Your Findings

Organizing what nursing science knows about a clinical problem and what you have discovered in the scientific literature is a common writing challenge, both for novices and experts. Accordingly, we suggest some strategies for arranging the relevant knowledge. Each strategy provides a unique emphasis to meet your audience and purpose, but each strategy also has its unique drawback. Among the common organizational patterns are:

Chronological order

Arranging the research evidence in the order in which it was discovered and published.

- *Advantage*: Use this order when you want to show the developmental evolution of the science.
- *Disadvantage*: This order may give a false impression of linear development while ignoring earlier blind alleys that could be promising later.

Research design typology order

Arranging the evidence according to the types of studies (e.g., quantitative designs/qualitative designs/mixed-methods designs, or by types within one [e.g., phenomenological, grounded theory, or ethnographic among qualitative designs]).

- *Advantage*: Use this order when you want to discuss generalizability among quantitative studies and transferability among qualitative studies, as well as showing relationships between study designs' findings.
- *Disadvantage*: This order may compartmentalize studies in a way that prevents you from showing how different studies might engage in conversation with each other.

Weakest to strongest studies order
Arranging evidence according to design rigor, sample size, or effect size.

- *Advantage*: Use this order's "crescendo effect" to stimulate growing confidence while your audience or reader follows your argument.
- *Disadvantage*: This order may confuse sample size with significance.

Weakest to strongest evidence order
Arranging evidence according to its persuasiveness in supporting your thesis.

- *Advantage*: Use this "crescendo effect" to stimulate growing confidence in your argument.
- *Disadvantage*: This order may give rise to your own confirmation bias or the cherry picking of data in which you ignore conflicting or ambiguous studies.

Thematic order
Arranging evidence according to the themes that emerge from various studies.

- *Advantage*: Use this order when you want to show commonalities among disparate studies by different researchers or at different times.
- *Disadvantage*: This order might entail forced categorization that does not withstand careful scrutiny; it may also involve trying to squeeze different studies into artificial groupings.

Once you've organized what we know about a phenomenon, it's time for you to describe what we do *not* know. As we explained in Chapter 2, identifying gaps in our knowledge is important because it prevents you and your readers from jumping to conclusions, and it opens the door for further research.

Revise Early Drafts

Print out a hard copy of your draft. (Copy editors usually work from hard copies, and we have observed that we more frequently find weaknesses and inconsistencies in our writing when we copyedit or proofread a paper version.) Let a day or two go by, and then reread it. Does it logically and clearly flow from one section to another? If you are a graduate student, your nursing professors will expect you to employ the far more detailed and complicated literature review process called *PRISMA*. In 2009 the Public Library of Science (PLoS Medicine) developed the PRISMA guidelines (a convenient acronym for *Preferred Reporting Items for Systematic Reviews and Meta-Analyses*), which outline how you should explain and document your review process of the literature. This includes both a detailed flow diagram to document the decisions that you made during the process of reviewing the literature and a table of specific criteria for evaluation. You can find this process and criteria at the PRISMA website: http://www .prisma-statement.org.

Organizing Your Literature Review

If you are writing either an integrative review or a systematic review, your report should begin with an introduction stating the purpose of your review, followed by a section on the methodology of your review. This description can help readers of your review assess the rigor you used (McGrath, 2012). You should describe the databases you searched, your criteria for including and excluding studies, how you reviewed the studies, and how you synthesized the findings.

Although literature reviews are likely to share certain structural features (e.g., a description of the methods used to search the literature), how you arrange the discussion of the research literature will depend on a variety of factors. You cannot predict exactly how your literature review will be organized before you obtain all the relevant studies from your search.

You might have identified twenty or thirty (or more) studies. How do you organize them coherently? Visually arranging them in groups is helpful, which you can do in digital electronic sorting or in hard copies arranged in piles. Tom Long recommends using your computer's desktop view to arrange PDF file icons in groups that you sort. Make sure to develop a file-naming protocol so that you can readily recognize each by name. Cheryl Beck recommends that you print out hard copies of your studies so you can sort them physically into piles. Each pile will ultimately become a section of your literature review. However, regardless of the method, sorting studies into these piles is an iterative process. Some original piles may need to be combined, while other piles may need to be divided into two or more piles. The piles of articles can be then physically arranged in the order in which you will write them up in the literature review. This visual framework will help you organize many different research articles in various combinations until you find the structure that seems most congruent.

In a literature review you identify a *phenomenon* and you ask a *research question*. For example: *Research has shown that cardiac rehabilitation after acute coronary syndromes can significantly reduce the recurrence of coronary events, but low enrollment in rehabilitation programs is common* (that's a *phenomenon*). *Why, then, is there such low enrollment in cardiac rehabilitation programs?* (that's a *research question*).

Suppose you wanted to test an intervention to increase patients' enrollment in cardiac rehabilitation after discharge from the hospital. Prior to developing such an intervention, you would need to review the relevant literature on cardiac rehabilitation. Reviewing the literature, you would locate studies that tested different kinds of interventions to increase enrollment in cardiac rehabilitation, like automatic referrals or liaisons involving personal contact between cardiac patients and clinicians.

How should you approach the writing of the results of your literature review? One option for organizing is by first reviewing the studies pertaining to the independent variable (the intervention [i.e., cardiac rehabilitation enrollment programs]) followed by a review of the studies measuring the dependent variable (the outcome [i.e., enrollment]). Then the cardiac rehabilitation intervention studies can be organized in various ways, for instance by (1) type of intervention (to compare different intervention modes), (2) studies that had significant findings versus those that had nonsignificant findings (to establish a hierarchy of effectiveness), or (3) chronological order (to demonstrate a development of different approaches over time). Once the research on the independent variable has been summarized, then you can concentrate on the studies that measured the dependent variable.

Sometimes in a literature review the purpose is to summarize the measurement of a key variable, such as postpartum depression. After gathering the studies using different screening scales, you find that a number of different scales have been used to measure postpartum depressive symptoms (e.g. Edinburgh Postnatal Depression Scale and the Postpartum Depression Screening Scale). Again, organized stacks of the articles (either on your computer's desktop view or in physical piles in hard copies) can facilitate your organization of the review of literature. Stacks can be made of studies using each specific scale. Perhaps as you review the studies in each pile, you can sort them further by the population sampled (e.g., age group or cultural group). In the literature review you would need to identify the psychometrics of each scale for each study.

The table or matrix for which we provided a template in Figure 6.1 above is extremely helpful here. Having each study assigned its own row with columns identifying common characteristics of studies will enable you to compare and contrast the studies.

Guidelines for Synthesizing Studies

In our digital, online, cut-and-paste world, the biggest weakness of novice nurse writers is the tendency simply to string together different studies without cogently synthesizing them. *A literature review is not just a series of article critiques or reviews.* Such a "patchwork quilt" or "string of pearls" approach fails to show the relationships among studies or to demonstrate their relative strengths, weaknesses, and relevance. In our experience, novice writers may be able to summarize information (i.e., "review" it in a rather passive sense) but are less skilled at synthesizing information—which is the more active version of "reviewing" that you should be aiming for. Here we suggest some guidelines for helping you synthesize a variety of complex studies.

How to Show Relationships Among Diverse Studies

Cluster articles with similar research designs (e.g., quantitative studies with other quantitative studies, qualitative studies with other qualitative studies, mixed-methods studies with other mixed-methods studies).

How to Assess Conflicting Findings

Analyze the studies for differences in their research designs that might account for the conflicting findings. Discuss and evaluate weaker study designs before turning to the stronger studies.

How to Anticipate Readers' Objections

Acknowledge and accurately represent objections that have already been made or that might be made before turning to respond to each objection.

How to Present Alternatives While Emphasizing Your Recommendation

Acknowledge that there is not universal agreement on a desired course of action and accurately represent the alternatives before turning to identify the alternatives' weaknesses and your recommendation's strengths.

How to Argue in Support of an Implementation and Evaluation Plan

After synthesizing the literature thematically or integratively with particular attention to the causes, associations, and correlations of a phenomenon or intervention, demonstrate the

Headings or No Headings?

Some literature reviews—especially the longer ones—are divided into sections, and each section has a heading. Those headings make the organization explicit to readers. Other reviews, like the one below, rely on topic sentences and transitions instead of headings to guide the reader.

ways that your proposal addresses most or even all of those factors.

Going Beyond the Basics

Below is an example of how one nursing student went beyond a cut-and-paste or series-of-summaries approach to the quantitative literature on fear of childbirth in women with a history of sexual abuse. She provided her readers with a description of her search procedure and then identified a global picture of her results: that only a few quantitative studies were located on this topic. When the nursing student described the quantitative studies looking at fear during labor, she presented the conflicting findings among studies, which revealed that some of the studies found a significant relationship between exposure to violence and fear of childbirth while other studies reported a nonsignificant relationship. This student ended her review with a summary paragraph that highlighted the conflicting findings from the quantitative studies and observed the limitation that these studies were not conducted in the United States. Through her literature review, she built a systematic case for why additional research was needed.

Literature Review for Fear of Childbirth in Women with a History of Sexual Abuse

An extensive literature review took place using CINAHL, PsycINFO and PubMed. Given the lack of scholarly articles on this topic, the quantitative literature review included articles from 1990 to current 2013 publications. Quantitative studies examining fear of childbirth were identified, and three specifically examined this construct in survivors of sexual violence (Heimstad et al., 2006; Lukasse et al., 2010; Schroll et al., 2011).

> The first paragraph presents the search procedure, including the databases searched and the date range of articles consulted (one of her inclusion criteria). She also summarizes the *number* and *kinds* of studies to be included in the review.

To date, there are only a few studies that quantitatively examine fear of childbirth in women with a history of sexual abuse. Furthermore, these few published studies have conflicting results despite use of the same instrument, the Wijma Delivery Expectancy/Experience Questionnaire (W-DEQ). Recent research on this topic "showed no association between exposure to violence and fear of childbirth before or during labor" (Schroll et al., 2011, p. 22). In this study, women with a history of sexual violence reported a fear of childbirth only after delivery (Schroll et al., 2011). Conversely, research where the W-DEQ was given during pregnancy demonstrated a correlation between a childhood history of physical, emotional, or sexual abuse, and fear of childbirth (Heimstad et al., 2006; Lukasse et al., 2010). The timing of the questionnaire's administration may account for the variance in these study results.

> Notice how three different studies are cited in this single paragraph because they all fall under the subheading. Also note how transitional words ("Conversely, . . .") signal clear relationships between them.

> Citing two studies with similar results at the end of single sentence is more efficient (and sophisticated) than creating two separate sentences.

Schroll et al. (2011) conducted the most recent research on this topic, examining the prevalence of sexual violence and if women with this history have a higher risk of fear of childbirth before, during, or after delivery. The study was conducted in Denmark with

2,638 low-risk primiparous women using the W-DEQ. Nearly 10% of the sample (9.2%) had experienced sexual violence. The results demonstrated "no association between exposure to violence and fear of childbirth before or during labor" (Schroll et al., 2011, p. 22). However, women with a history of sexual violence experienced an increased risk for severe fear of childbirth (defined as W-DEQ score >84) after delivery when compared to women who never experienced sexual violence, odds ratio 1.5 (95% CI: 1.02–2.27) (Schroll et al., 2011). Theoretically, survivors may repress their history of violence during pregnancy but then experience flashbacks to the abuse during delivery, thus causing increased fear postpartum.

In contrast, Eberhard-Gran et al. (2008) examined if fear during labor was associated with sexual abuse in adult life. The study was conducted with women six weeks postpartum (N = 414) in Norway; however, it did not use the W-DEQ.

Here the writer introduces a new subtopic, one that highlights the key difference in the researchers' choices of instruments to assess fear of labor, which can significantly affect the findings.

Instead, a 3-point scale of "no fear, some fear, or extreme fear" measured participants' fear. One third of the women experiencing extreme fear during labor had a history of sexual violence, odds ratio 3.7 (95% CI: 1.0–3.7). The contrasting findings of Eberhard-Gran et al. (2008) and Schroll et al. (2011) are most likely due to the difference in data collection instruments.

Again the writer cites two closely related studies (in this case with contrasting findings) in a single sentence and gives details of how they are related.

In Norway, Heimstad et al. (2006) administered the W-DEQ to 1,452 women at 18 weeks gestation in order to assess the prevalence of fear of childbirth and to examine an association of fear with sociodemographic characteristics. The overall prevalence of serious fear of childbirth (defined as a W-DEQ score >100) was 5.5%. Women with a history of childhood sexual abuse had a higher score (71) on the W-DEQ than non-abused women

(61, $p < 0.01$). Contrasting Schroll et al.'s (2011) findings, Heimstad et al. (2006) found exposure to sexual abuse as a child, but not as an adult, was associated with fear of childbirth. Heimstad et al. (2006) also found that a history of childhood sexual abuse, not fear of childbirth, negatively influenced the mode of delivery: "Among those who reported exposure to physical and sexual abuse in childhood, only 57% and 54% respectively, had uncomplicated vaginal deliveries at term, compared to 75% among those who did not report abuse ($p < 0.001$)" (Heimstad et al., 2006, p. 438).

Lukasse et al. (2010) examined if there was an association between a history of childhood abuse and fear of childbirth in a cross-sectional study of 2,365 women in Norway. The W-DEQ was administered after 18 weeks gestation and severe fear of childbirth was defined as a score of 85 or more. They observed, "Women with a history of childhood abuse reported severe fear of childbirth significantly more often than those without a history of childhood abuse, 18% versus 10% ($p = 0.001$)" (Lukasse et al., 2010, p. 267). Lukasse et al.'s (2010) findings resonate with those of Heimstad et al. (2006).

This writer rightly summarizes or paraphrases nearly all her sources, but the occasional direct quotation is also fitting.

As part of a larger study examining a relationship between anxiety sensitivity and fear of childbirth, Spice, Jones, Hadjistavropoulos, Kowalyk, and Stewart (2009) administered the W-DEQ to 110 pregnant women in Canada. Similar to previous studies, 9.1% of the sample experienced extreme fear of childbirth (defined W-DEQ score ≥ 85). Primiparous women were more likely to experience fear of childbirth. In this study, the internal consistency coefficient for the W-DEQ was .91.

Transitional phrases, such as "Similar to previous studies," signal that the writer is engaging in synthesis— that she sees the big picture.

Research by Alehagen, Wijma, and Wijma (2006) in Sweden explored the association between fear of childbirth during pregnancy and postpartum, and fear and pain during early labor. Women who received epidural anesthesia in labor were compared to those who did not. The W-DEQ was administered to 47 nulliparous women at 37–39 weeks gestation, the Delivery Fear Scale was administered during early labor, and the W-DEQ was again administered 2 hours, two days, and five weeks postpartum. The findings "show a relationship between fear of childbirth experienced during late pregnancy, early active labor, and the postpartum period" but are not specific to women with a history of sexual abuse (Alehagen, Wijma, & Wijma, 2006, p. 56). Additionally, no difference was found in fear of childbirth during pregnancy between the women who received epidural anesthesia versus those who did not; however, the women who received epidural anesthesia reported more fear postpartum. An epidural can slow down labor, which Alehagen et al. (2006) hypothesize is the reason these women experienced more fear postpartum.

Ryding, Wijma, and Wijma (1998) utilized the W-DEQ (shortened 20-item version B) to compare the psychological reactions of primiparous and multiparous women in Sweden after emergency cesarean section, elective cesarean section, instrument vaginal delivery, and normal spontaneous vaginal delivery. All participants (N = 326) completed the W-DEQ a few days postpartum and at 1 month postpartum, with researchers finding at both time points that the emergency cesarean section group had the most negative appraisal of the delivery, followed by the instrument vaginal delivery group. Both of these groups experienced more post-traumatic stress, relative to the elective cesarean and normal spontaneous vaginal delivery groups.

Wiklund, Edman, Ryding, and Andolf (2008) examined the expectations and experiences of childbirth by cesarean section in primiparous women. This prospective, group-comparison cohort study took place in Sweden and compared primiparous women (N = 496) who had elective cesarean, cesarean for breech, and controls planning a vaginal delivery. The participants completed the W-DEQ prior to delivery and at 3 months postpartum. The results demonstrated that 43.4% of the mothers choosing an elective cesarean had negative expectations of a vaginal birth. Overall, mothers in the planned vaginal delivery group who instead had an emergency cesarean or an instrument-assisted vaginal birth reported the most negative experiences of childbirth. This finding is consistent with Ryding et al. (1998). Both Ryding et al. (1998) and Wiklund et al. (2008) recommend more postpartum follow-up and services for women undergoing emergency cesarean and instrument-assisted vaginal deliveries.

When multiple sources concur on the same or similar recommendations, alert your readers to that fact, as the writer does here.

The quantitative state of the science has conflicting results, making the findings difficult to apply in clinical practice. Moreover, these studies addressing fear of childbirth have been conducted in Norway, Denmark, and Sweden; therefore, the results may not correlate to the same cohort of women in the United States. Women experiencing fear of childbirth represent a vulnerable group (Ryding, Persson, Onell, & Kvist, 2003). As a result, more research in this content area is needed to improve the childbearing experiences of women in United States, as well as those abroad.

This paragraph summarizes the state of knowledge regarding quantitative research and ends with the rationale for why additional research is needed.

Again, thoughtful arrangement of information and ideas is the key to your writing with clarity, emphasis, and persuasive power. Most importantly, the literature review *evaluates* the studies and *synthesizes* the knowledge according to its relevant merits.

You will also want to consult sections of Chapter 10 that offer advice on several subskills essential to working with sources—summarizing and paraphrasing, positioning sources into your explanation or argument, and integrating sources into your writing—as well as the sections on APA citation conventions. Additional handbooks are available on writing literature reviews, and we recommend Galvan (2014) and Ling Pan (2013).

7

ADVOCACY WRITING, CLINICAL PRACTICE GUIDELINES/ARTICLES, AND CONFERENCE PROPOSALS

In academic settings most of your writing has narrow audiences and purposes (typically, showing your professors that you have mastered nurses' knowledge and thinking), but in the professional world you face a variety of audiences with a mixture of purposes and levels of understanding. Here we explore ways in which you might demonstrate your clinical expertise by advocating on behalf of health policy issues, vulnerable populations, or the nursing profession.

What Is Advocacy Writing?

The nursing profession takes pride in the fact that, for the past two decades of Gallup polling, Americans have identified nurses as the most ethical professionals (with physicians further down the list). However, does Americans' trust in ethical nurses also mean that they think of nurses as health authorities? Unfortunately, popular culture falls back on easy stereotypes of nurses, so when members of the news media need experts on health, they typically rely on contacts with physicians, not nurses.

This discrepancy between the perceived ethics of nurses and their perceived authority is well documented. In an examination of nurses' voices in the news media, Buresh, Gordon, and Bell (1991) found a substantial gap between physicians' and nurses' representations, which Buresh and Gordon (2000) saw persisting a decade later. The title of their book, *From Silence to Voice: What Nurses Know and Must Communicate to the Public*, suggests an important challenge for nurses, one that we would like to help you take up. Public advocacy writing— letters to the editor, editorials, op-ed essays (so called because they usually appear opposite the editorial page of a newspaper), and public hearing testimony—is one way for you to share your professional expertise and assert your authority.

Although many professional journals in nursing and other health sciences, as well as peer-reviewed science journals, publish editorials whose readership is fellow professionals (see Copp, 1997; Singh & Singh, 2006; Fontanarosa, 2014), our emphasis in this chapter is writing opinion pieces for general non-expert audiences. Admittedly, making the effort to craft a written response to a current issue in a timely fashion may seem overwhelming and the rewards seem elusive. Clinical nurses and administrators may be pressed for time and may even feel under some scrutiny by their employers when appearing in public debates about controversial issues. Further, the sheer number of opinion pieces that an editor receives means that the probability of yours being published might be small. However, you need to ensure that your expertise, professional role, and clear expression of a viewpoint will earn you publication.

Credibility: Have you provided accurate information?

Care: Have you engaged the reader emotionally to share your concern for your topic?

Competence: Have you assembled your information in a reasonable argument?

Novice writers need to keep several things in mind about advocacy writing. First, your response must be timely and relevant. Newspapers and other media may state a time limit on responses (e.g., responses to previously published editorials or articles must be submitted within seven days of the original article's appearance in print), so make sure that you understand what that deadline might be. Second, even if your letter, editorial, or op-ed piece is not published, don't be discouraged. Your submission serves an important function by educating the editorial page editor. Third, if you are responding to the work of a reporter or columnist, send a copy of your response to that writer as well. Journalists, like editors, also need to be educated about nursing. They often do not know what nurses do or how they can offer a unique perspective on health issues. Finally, attend to the instructions provided by the news outlet (e.g., word limits, style expectations, how to submit the piece), even as you leverage any personal or professional connections that can help you get the attention of editors.

Letters to the Editor

Letters to the editor, editorials, and op-ed essays follow well-established structures. A letter to the editor, for example, typically begins by stating the context for your letter (identifying the controversy, event, previously published article, news report, editorial, or op-ed essay to which you are responding) and establishing your credibility (your professional role, credentials, or experience). You can make your argument in one or two points by offering an assertion and supporting it with relevant facts. Finally, you conclude with a call to action or a summary of your main idea.

Let's take as an example the scope of practice of advanced practice nurses (APRNs), which continues to be controversial in some states. If you are writing a letter to the editor in support of expanding the scope of practice:

1. Establish the context for your letter (the issue, article, report, editorial, or op-ed essay that you are responding to).

   > Your April 30 article by Jane Smith ("Physician Shortage Ahead") ignored a vital health care profession that is already filling primary care gaps.

2. Establish your credibility (credentials or experience).

   > As a clinical nurse for 25 years and a nurse educator for the past 15 years, I have seen how advanced practice registered nurses (APRNs) have for years provided primary care to children and adults, diagnosing illness and prescribing treatments.

3. Make your argument in one or two points by making an assertion and supporting it with facts.

   > APRNs are educated and clinically experienced to provide comprehensive health care in the front lines, helping families stay healthy with preventive care and being aggressive in treating illness. In 20 states they provide independent care at less cost than that of physicians, and they specialize in disease prevention and health promotion. According to a RAND estimate Massachusetts could save four to eight billion dollars over ten years with expanded roles for APRNs.

4. Conclude your letter with a call to action or a summary of your main idea.

   > Your readers are not well served by ignoring the essential role that nurses will play in the Affordable Care Act's expansion of health care, and future

articles on the impending crisis must take APRNs into account.

Op-Ed Essays

Longer editorials or op-ed essays expand on this structure. Because an essay is longer than a letter to the editor, you can devote more space to the introductory paragraph and develop your points in greater detail. An editorial or op-ed essay may be less time sensitive, though it still focuses on issues in the news or in your community. First, you establish the context for your op-ed essay with an attention-grabbing first paragraph by using (1) a striking statistic, unusual fact, or vivid example or anecdote, (2) a paradoxical statement, (3) a quotation, (4) a question, or (5) an analogy. You can also make your argument in two or three points by offering assertions supported by facts or examples. You conclude your essay with a call to action or a summary of your main idea, keeping in mind that people are typically persuaded more by stories than by facts. Facts are of course necessary to follow through on your commitments to evidence and competence, but they carry more force when married to a narrative—note that in everyday talk we speak even of hard journalistic reporting as news "stories."

Using the same nursing professional issue (expanding APRNs' scope of practice to the fullest extent of their education) but with a slightly different angle (the need for more nursing faculty to teach the next generation of APRNs), you could develop the op-ed essay in this way:

1. Establish the context for your op-ed essay with an attention-grabbing introductory paragraph:

   According to John W. Rowe, MD, a physician and professor of health policy at Columbia University, the Affordable Care Act (sometimes called "Obamacare") will create an enormous need for an additional 30,000 physicians by 2015 and 65,000 by 2025, a gap that could be filled by advanced practice registered nurses (APRNs). Dr. Rowe has noted, "Well-trained registered nurses with specialized qualifications who can make diagnoses, order tests and referrals, and write prescriptions, APRNs could provide a variety of services that primary care physicians now provide."

2. Next, establish your credibility (credentials or authority):

The next generation of APRNs that my colleagues at the University of Connecticut School of Nursing and I are educating today will help meet that need.

3. After that introduction, make your argument in two or three points by making assertions supported by facts:

Yet two obstacles stand in our way of meeting the needs that Dr. Rowe has highlighted. First, we need to recruit and prepare additional nursing faculty. We cannot simply increase our enrollments in APRN programs; our accrediting agencies stipulate the student-to-faculty ratio in order to ensure quality preparation. Second, we need to legislate in each state an expansion of scope of practice permitted to APRNs. As Dr. Rowe has observed, "Despite an urgent need and clear evidence that APRNs can complement and extend primary care providers' roles—without sacrificing quality of care—nurses are only permitted to practice independently to the full extent of their training and competence" in only 20 states and the District of Columbia. It's time for the remaining 30 states to expand APRNs' scope of practice.

4. Conclude your essay with a call to action or a summary of your main idea, but keep in mind that people are persuaded by stories more often than by facts:

> You already know how hard it can be today to get an appointment with a physician and how little time the physician can spend with you. Think about how much worse that will get in a few years when 30 million additional currently uninsured Americans become regular patients. However, a cadre of advanced practice nurses stands ready to provide you and your family with a full range of health care. Provide the faculty needed to grow their ranks and give them the authority to practice what they have been prepared to do.

Often op-eds are written in response to very specific legislative efforts. For example, early in 2014 the governor of Connecticut announced that he would present to the state's General Assembly legislation to allow APRNs to practice autonomously to the fullest extent of their education, experience, and certification. Almost immediately there was vocal and visible resistance from a variety of quarters, particularly physician organizations. Tom Long, who provides writing support services to the University of Connecticut School of Nursing, encouraged its dean and APRNs to formulate written responses. They began posting replies on news websites and submitting letters to the editor. Tom negotiated with the editor of the editorial page of the *Hartford Courant*, the state's newspaper of record, to publish an op-essay. In February 2014, the essay was published under the byline of Dean Regina Cusson and Director of Advanced Practice Programs Ivy Alexander, but it was the work of many hands, with the contribution of ideas and information from a variety of nursing faculty. You can read it if you Google the authors and the title, "Take Reins Off Advanced Practice Nurses." You'll notice that it includes the four basic structural features outlined above, although it runs longer. Also note how it begins with a specific reference to Governor Molloy's proposal (even as it notes the opposition to it by some "some critics") and ends with a recommendation to support the proposed law in the state legislature. The legislation eventually was approved in the General Assembly and was signed into law by the governor.

Hearing testimony given before a legislative or professional panel is structured similarly. In hearing settings you will typically be given a time limitation (three, five, or ten minutes is typical), so keep in mind that one typed, double-spaced page of twelve-point type usually takes two minutes to read. Depending on how much time you are accorded, expand or contract the overall length of your text.

Nurses' voices in the public sphere—drawing on their expertise and observations—are indispensable. Following this formula and adapting it as circumstances demand will make it easier for you to speak out with credibility, care, and competence on behalf of both your patients and your profession.

Clinical Practice Guidelines

Knowing the evidence base and its knowledge gaps and understanding their significance to nursing practice are essential habits of professional thought. How does the evidence base become implemented in nursing practice? One form of professional writing thus deserves your attention: clinical practice guidelines. In this form of writing and dissemination, you will not be working as a solo author or even as a co-author on a small team. Clinical practice guidelines are a collaborative effort requiring the participation of many stakeholders and health professionals. As Stevens (2013) observed, nursing science became a knowledge producer of this genre in the 1960s, but it was not until the 1990s that the need for dissemination and implementation of nursing science's evidence base became more urgent:

> To affect better patient outcomes, new knowledge must be transformed into clinically useful forms, effectively implemented across the entire care team within a systems context, and measured in terms of meaningful impact on performance and health outcomes. The recently-articulated vision for the future of nursing in the [Institute of Medicine's 2011] *Future of Nursing* report focuses on the convergence of knowledge, quality, and new functions in nursing. The recommendation that nurses lead interprofessional teams in improving delivery systems and care brings to the fore the necessity for new competencies, beyond evidence-based practice (EBP), that are requisite as nurses transform healthcare. These competencies focus on utilizing knowledge in clinical decision making and producing research evidence on interventions that promote uptake and use by individual providers and groups of providers.

As a nursing student or novice nurse, you will use clinical practice guidelines, but you will not be invited to participate in a clinical practice guideline committee or task force until you have become a highly experienced or advanced practice nurse.

Disseminating new knowledge for clinical implementation in nursing practice is the purpose of clinical practice guidelines.

> *Credibility*: Are you a member of a committee or task force whose members have appropriate expertise?
>
> *Care*: Have you considered how to overcome institutional and professional inertia in proposing new guidelines?
>
> *Competence*: Have you reviewed, evaluated, and synthesized the relevant clinical science?

A definition of clinical practice guidelines offered by the Institute of Medicine (IOM) (Graham et al., 2011, p. 15) is "statements that include recommendations intended to optimize patient care that are informed by a systematic review of evidence and assessment of the benefits and harms of alternative care options." The IOM has published eight standards for developing clinical practice guidelines to ensure their quality:

1. Establish transparency.
2. Manage conflicts of interest.
3. Develop guidelines for group composition.
4. Analyze intersections of clinical practice guidelines and systematic reviews.
5. Establish evidence foundations for and rating of strength of recommendations.
6. Articulate recommendations.
7. Conduct an external review.
8. Update every three to five years.

For the first standard, the developers of a clinical practice guideline need to describe the processes of how it was developed and identify any funding received. This transparency is needed to decrease bias and conflicts of interest. In the second, standard group members should declare any conflict of interest they may have. The third standard focuses on the composition of the team, which needs to be multidisciplinary and balanced—it should include experts, stakeholders, clinicians, and patients who will be affected by the guideline.

Systematic reviews are critical to developing these guidelines, which is the focus of the fourth standard. When reaching the fifth standard, the group members need to establish the evidence and strength of the evidence for their recommendations. Next, recommendations are articulated. In the seventh standard, an external review of the guidelines is done, with further updates every three to five years.

Because many clinical practice guidelines are available to you online, we provide you here with a sampling of the organizations that assemble them. The U.S. Agency for Healthcare Research and Quality (AHRQ) manages the National Guideline Clearinghouse. It organizes guidelines in a number of ways, including by topic or by professional organization. Nursing organizations are included, such as the Association of Women's Health, Obstetric, and Neonatal Nursing (AWHONN) and the Association of Perioperative Registered Nurses (AORN). Another resource is the Canadian Registered Nurses' Association of Ontario (RNAO).

Although formal evidence-based clinical practice guidelines are the product of a methodical and thorough consensus among interprofessional stakeholders, as a nursing student, and certainly as a nurse in practice, you will have opportunities for bringing your health organization and its practices up to date. For example, in the final semester of their baccalaureate degree program's clinical capstone, our seniors at the University of Connecticut engage in team projects for their clinical sites. These projects focus on health promotion and maintenance, basic care and comfort, infection prevention, or safety. Students' teams are evaluated according to how well they formulate a PICO question (patient problem or population; intervention; comparison; and outcomes), articulate the significance of the problem, search and synthesize the literature, make coherent evidence-based recommendations, and argue for the congruence of the change process theory they select. The teams prepare a poster presentation that they make at the school's annual research day and at their clinical capstone sites. Each team is essentially charged with composing a student version of an evidence-based clinical practice guideline.

Clinical Practice Articles

In introducing the clinical practice article in Chapter 1, we observed that in this genre clinical nurses share with other clinical nurses fresh understandings of patient needs and nursing care regarding a particular health concern or disease. The idea for writing a clinical practice article may come from your own experience in providing care to a patient. The clinical practice article might focus on a nursing intervention that was extremely successful or maybe one that was frustrating. You might also highlight issues that you encountered in providing nursing care and how you resolved those issues.

Oermann and Hays (2010, p. 166) identified some questions you should ask yourself when you are considering writing a clinical practice article:

- "Is the idea new and innovative?
- If the idea is not new, does it provide a different perspective to current practice?
- Is the content relevant to clinical practice, and if so, is it applicable to nursing practice in a specialty area or in general?
- Do nurses need this information for their practice and will it improve patient care?

- Will the information be valuable in keeping nurses up-to-date about trends in nursing and healthcare?
- Will the content inform readers about the types of activities and work nurses are doing in other settings and places?"

Saver (2011) lists some of the elements that a clinical article might include: etiology, pathophysiology, incidence, clinical presentation, differential diagnoses, diagnostics, treatment/interventions/medications, patient education, prevention, and nursing implications.

Once you decide on the topic of your article, you need to be clear on its purpose. For instance, are you describing a different perspective to the usual nursing practice? Are you describing the effectiveness of using a clinical practice guideline with patients? Or are you focusing on an interdisciplinary plan of care that worked well with your patients? (Oermann & Hays, 2010). You also need to consider who your audience will be for your clinical article: Nurses in general? A specific specialty of nursing? Nursing educators? Nursing students? Your intended audience will influence the article's length and degree of technical language.

One way to start is with a case scenario to grab the attention of the reader. This can be an anecdotal description of your experience with a patient. Oermann and Hays (2010, p. 171) suggest starting a clinical practice article with a paragraph that

Credibility: Have you demonstrated your own informed clinical skill?

Care: Have you provided your readers with insights that are new and significant?

Competence: Have you provided information that is new and significant?

places the reader in a clinical situation: "You describe a scenario in nursing practice and ask the reader, what would you do in this situation?" Another approach to starting your clinical practice article can be to provide current statistics regarding the issue or disease, which can convince your readers that the topic is important.

Saver (2011) suggests starting a clinical practice article by creating a simple outline with about four to six key areas you want to cover. Making a bulleted list of ideas is helpful. This outline will provide a guide for you as you are writing so that you will not drift off from the topic. Saver (2011, p. 179) offers a seven-step approach to writing a strong clinical practice article:

- "Develop a clinical topic and focus.
- Select a journal for publication
- Choose an appropriate format
- Gather information.
- Write using active voice.
- Edit your manuscript.
- Submit!"

In the main portion of your article you can provide examples from your clinical practice to help the readers apply the new material to their nursing care, be it assessment of patients, diagnostic tests, patient responses, nursing interventions, or outcomes. Oermann and Hays (2010) also offer some guidelines for writing the body of a clinical practice article, which we summarize here:

- When writing up the content go from simple to complex, and from what is known to what is not known.
- Make sure you include background information to allow the reader to understand the rationale for interventions or outcomes.

- Concentrate on what is essential for nurses to know regarding assessing their patients, the relevant diagnostic testing, and interventions.
- Concentrate on nursing management and not medical management.
- Include examples from your clinical practice to illustrate points you are making.
- Remember that the content of your clinical practice article depends on the background of the readers so that content is written at an appropriate level.

When revising your manuscript, it is important to obtain feedback from colleagues who are familiar with your topic.

Conference Proposals

Even as nursing students you have important observations and insights about health care. When you become a nurse, those insights can deepen.

The world needs you to tell it what you know. You might do this via a letter to the editor, an editorial, or an op-ed essay to a publication for a mass audience, but you might also make a poster presentation or a podium presentation at a professional conference to an audience of health care providers. Many

Credibility: Have you selected a conference or publication appropriate to your topic?
Care: Have you demonstrated the significance of your findings?
Competence: Does your proposal abstract or manuscript conform to the expectations of the conference organizers or publication editors?

universities host a parallel version of this: on-campus under-graduate research conferences, which invite students to share their research in posters or podium presentations. You might also submit a manuscript for publication in a research or professional journal. Each form of dissemination has its own processes and genre expectations.

Increasingly, undergraduate honors students as well as graduate students are encouraged to disseminate their research findings at conferences as either a podium or a poster presentation. For example, at its annual scientific sessions the Eastern Nursing Research Society holds a poster competition for undergraduate students. These various ways to disseminate findings require writing a proposal abstract, which is a condensed version of an entire completed (or ongoing) research study or project that succinctly describes the key elements.

Before we discuss abstracts any further, we need to clear up something that could be confusing. In general, *abstract* refers to any summary of a study, essay, article, or manuscript. In a research literature database, you will often find a summary of each article called an abstract. When you read a research article, you will often find on its first page a paragraph or a structured outline called an abstract, which summarizes the main points of the article. Here we are using *abstract* in another sense, and to try to make that clearer, we will call it a *proposal abstract*. In other words, it's a summary of a poster or a podium presentation that you are proposing to give at a conference.

The proposal abstract presents the bare bones of your research study or clinical project. It contains the material you would like to present at a conference. The main purpose of a proposal abstract is to help conference organizers make a decision on whether to accept your presentation for the conference. Sometimes the accepted abstracts are published in the conference proceedings.

A publicized "call for abstracts" from organizers of research or clinical conferences includes important information. It specifies rules and instructions for abstract submission. Some of the usual guidelines provided by conference organizers include the following:

- Main theme or topic of the conference
- Deadline for submission
- Type of abstracts to be considered
- Format required: structured abstract versus unstructured abstract
- Abstract length (word limit, font style)
- Project status: completed versus in-progress research
- Previously presented or not

Conferences often have a main theme, and most proposal abstracts should speak in some way to that theme. For example, the theme for the 26th Annual Scientific Sessions for Eastern Nursing Research Society was "Promoting Health Across the Life Span: The Art and Science of Person-Centered Care." Thus proposal abstracts should have been framed with that theme in mind.

The conference organizers' deadline for submission of a proposal abstract is critical. Sometimes conference organizers may extend the deadline, but you cannot count on this. All your hard work writing an abstract will be for naught if you try to submit it once the deadline has passed.

Look carefully at the call for abstracts or call for proposals to see if the type of proposal abstract you want to submit is being considered for the conference. Common proposal abstract types are research-related abstracts, theoretical abstracts (e.g., a concept analysis), systematic reviews of literature, clinical practice projects, education projects, and quality improvement projects (Linder, 2012).

Effective Titles

A title that indicates the results of a study is more interesting than a general title. For example, a general title like "The Effect of a Diet Involved with DHA During Pregnancy on Postpartum Depressive Symptoms" tells you the topic but nothing else. Is there a positive effect? A negative effect? No effect? A small effect? A more specific title instead would read "DHA Supplementation During Pregnancy Reduces Postpartum Depressive Symptoms in New Mothers." Now the reader knows that your presentation is going to include findings of positive health outcomes.

Depending on the conference, the abstracts may have to be written in either structured or unstructured formats. A *structured format* will call for using specific subheadings, such as *Purpose, Background, Methods, Results, Conclusions*, and *Implications for Clinical Practice*, while an *unstructured abstract* is written as one continuous paragraph without any subheadings (although it should include the same information as a structured abstract but without the display of subheadings). The abstract length involves not only the word limit (usually between 250 and 300 words) but also font size (usually twelve-point type).

Next you need to check the guidelines for abstract submission to see if the conference organizers will only accept proposal abstracts of completed research or if they will also entertain abstracts of ongoing research. Ongoing research would only be considered for poster presentations and not a full podium paper presentation.

Lastly, some conferences will accept abstracts only if the work included in the abstract has not been previously presented at any other conference. Those conference organizers only want "breaking news" that no one has seen publicly before.

Now let's concentrate on the proposal abstract's content. Components of the content (regardless of whether it is a structured or unstructured abstract) include the following:

Title
Include the main variables, the sample, the setting, and the design.

Background
This alerts readers as to why your topic is important. Write it concisely to build a convincing argument for the merit of the research problem addressed in your study. Sometimes "Background" and "Purpose" are combined.

Purpose
State clearly the purpose of your study and indicate the scope of your research. This only takes one sentence, which typically begins, "The purpose of this study was . . ."

Methods
Describe the research, its design and theoretical framework, sample, key variables, instruments used to collect data, and data analysis.

Results
Key findings are the focus of this section. Be specific. If your study was quantitative and you found significant results, include the statistical values along with the p values. Avoid vague general statements, and provide specific data-driven findings.

In qualitative studies, the results you describe should be consistent with the research design of the study. For instance, if it is a grounded theory study, the findings should not be written up as themes.

Conclusion
Your conclusions must be supported by the data, but be careful not to overstate the significance of the data. In this section you address the implications for clinical practice and often make suggestions for future research.

Here is an example of a proposal abstract by one of our students using a structured format.

Variations in Undergraduate Nursing Students' Test Anxiety Levels Correlated with Year and GPA

Background/Purpose:

For many undergraduate nursing students, performing well in required coursework is important. However, nursing students often face pressure-filled academic situations, and worrying about them may inhibit their ability to demonstrate actual knowledge of course material. This can, in turn, interfere with students completing their undergraduate programs or with choosing to pursue advanced nursing degrees following graduation. The purpose of this study was to assess and compare test anxiety levels of sophomore and senior undergraduate nursing students.

continued

continued

Methods:

A convenience sample was utilized for this descriptive survey. A total of 219 nursing students completed a scale that consisted of 26 statements focusing on the cognitive domain of test anxiety. Scores could range from 26 to 104, with higher values indicating greater anxiety. Three cut-points were applied to define low (26–59), moderate (60–69), and high (70–104) anxiety groups.

Results:

Internal validity of the instrument was supported by a Cronbach's alpha of 0.94. The total mean score was $M = 67.5$ ($SD = \pm 15.03$) and corresponded to a moderate level of anxiety. Mean score comparisons were conducted and showed a sophomore ($N = 111$) mean anxiety level of 71.2 ($SD = \pm 14.39$) and a senior ($N = 108$) anxiety level of 63.6 ($SD = \pm 14.77$). The sophomore and senior anxiety levels were significantly different ($p < .001$). Mean score comparisons between male ($M = 66.04$, $SD \pm 14.24$, $N = 23$) and female ($M = 67.64$, $SD = \pm 15.16$, $N = 193$) students revealed no significant difference ($p = 0.61$). Students who had a GPA below 3.0 had significantly higher anxiety levels ($M = 83.3$) than students who reported a GPA above 3.0 ($M = 66.4$, $p < .001$).

Conclusion:

Overall, nursing students have moderate to high test anxiety levels. Sophomore nursing students have higher mean levels than senior students and students who have a GPA below 3.0 have higher levels than those with a GPA above 3.0. There was no difference in anxiety between male and female students. Strategies that improve managing test anxiety, such as early assessment, increased awareness, and providing anxiety-reducing interventions for students, may be appropriate additions to undergraduate nursing curricula.

The world needs to hear what nurses know. Your clinical expertise, your perspective on holistic health, and your ethical commitment to health care equity for vulnerable populations need to be part of public debates.

THINKING AND COMMUNICATING VISUALLY

Tables, Figures, Presentation Slides, and Posters

A discussion of visual displays of information may seem like an odd topic for a guide to nursing writing until you remember that Florence Nightingale was both a skilled statistician and a keen proponent of effective visuals. Her classic polar figure showing month-by-month causes of mortality during the Crimean War has both clarity and impact (see Figure 8.1). The lightly shaded segments represent death by war wounds, the darker gray segments deaths by what we now call *infectious diseases*, the black segments deaths by other causes. It makes the argument forcefully that disease, rather than military trauma, was the leading cause of death over time.

A *table* is any tabulated display of data (numbers or words) in labeled columns and rows.

A *figure* is any other visual display, including graphs, charts, photographs, line drawings, maps, or schematic diagrams.

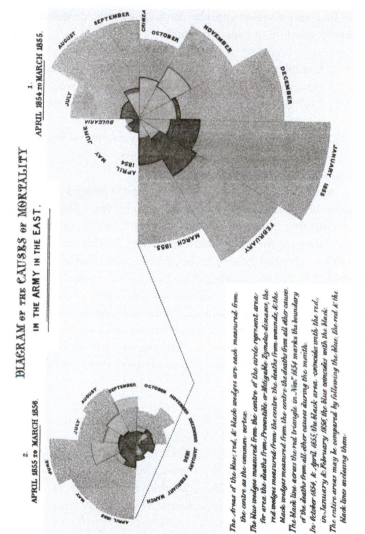

FIGURE 8.1 Florence Nightingale's polar chart of deaths during the Crimean War.

In a single visual apprehension, this figure demonstrates several qualities of effective visuals:

1. Complex data and their relationships are depicted (incidence of wounds, diseases, multiple causes).
2. Multiple dimensions are shown (causes of death, periods of time).
3. Size or scale of the segments provides visual impact to show the significance of phenomena.

A comprehensive discussion of visuals is beyond the scope of our brief guide, but this chapter will offer you a short primer on visual presentations of data—that is, how to create visuals and integrate them with text. Foremost, in this section you will learn how to present tables, graphs, and illustrations embedded in papers or other documents, like research posters, which nursing students and nurses also often use to display literature reviews or new findings. In addition, we will examine effective ways of using presentation software like PowerPoint or Prezi when you are making podium or classroom presentations. Finally, we will provide guidelines for the visual arrangement of posters.

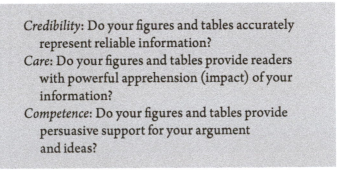

Credibility: Do your figures and tables accurately represent reliable information?

Care: Do your figures and tables provide readers with powerful apprehension (impact) of your information?

Competence: Do your figures and tables provide persuasive support for your argument and ideas?

Decide When a Visual Is Needed

There are two things to consider when trying to determine if visual displays are needed: *expectation* and *effect*.

Expectation

What does your audience expect? In some kinds of reports, literature reviews, and other genres, readers will expect you to use either figures or tables or both. Your understanding of the conventions (rules, expectations) of a particular kind of presentation or writing will guide you. In addition, specific audiences typically expect certain kinds of visuals. For example, more technically expert audiences, like researchers and clinicians, often expect certain kinds of data to be displayed in tables. In quantitative research papers, statistical tables and graphs are often expected; in literature reviews, a table of the articles reviewed may be expected.

Effect

How do you want to inform or persuade your audience or readers beyond the prose of the written text? Is there an effect produced by a figure or table that cannot be produced by sentences and paragraphs? Visuals show things beyond the power of words to tell, particularly in a visually mediated culture like ours. Table 8.1 offers guidance on the kind of visuals you may choose to produce a specific effect.

Choose the Most Fitting Type of Visual

In general, we distinguish between two types of figures: charts and graphs, or photographs and drawings. Charts and graphs represent relationships among categories of data: parts to the whole, trends over time, relative differences among phenomena, locations. Photographs and drawings provide

TABLE 8.1   Common Types of Visuals Used in Nursing Writing

When you want to:	You should use:
Display numbers Show repetitive data Display raw or processed data Present words for themes, concepts, or technical terms	Tables
Show trends over time and relationships among different phenomena	Line graph
Show comparisons and contrasts among datasets	Bar graph
Show parts-to-whole relationships	Pie graph
Show a work plan with milestones, their chronological sequence, and the projected amount of time each will require (frequently used in research proposals)	Gantt chart

representations of visually observed phenomena. For example, in a literature review, you might choose to include a chart demonstrating the frequency of research published on your topic over a two-decade period or a photograph of the manifestations of a disease.

Tables

Tables might seem boring—they don't bring flash or color—but remember that the main job of visuals is to be functional, not decorative. Tables are the optimal choice when you expect your audience will need to find individual values or compare individual values. See, for example, Table 8.2. They're also often the right choice when you have only a few data points, or when values involve multiple units of measure, or even when the information is verbal and not numerical. Notice

TABLE 8.2   States with the Highest Employment Levels
             in Nursing

State	Employment	Employment per thousand jobs	Location quotient	Hourly mean wage	Annual mean wage
California	253,310	16.75	0.84	$47.31	$98,400
Texas	190,170	16.94	0.85	$32.98	$68,590
New York	169,560	19.24	0.97	$37.07	$77,110
Florida	163,950	21.39	1.08	$30.15	$62,720
Pennsylvania	128,750	22.77	1.15	$32.01	$66,570

Adapted from U.S. Department of Labor Bureau of Labor Statistics, Occupational Employment and Wages, May 2014, 29-1141 Registered Nurses. Retrieved from http://www.bls.gov/oes/current/oes291141.htm#st

that Table 8.1 works well for all of those last three reasons. Table 8.2 illustrates how tables can represent numerical, statistical information.

Graphs and Charts

Line graphs

Line graphs represent trends over time, with the horizontal axis showing time and the vertical axis showing relative quantification. In Figure 8.2 you see how enrollment (the vertical axis) has risen fairly steadily since the mid-1980s (the horizontal axis). These data could be represented in a bar graph, too (with a bar for each data point), but the line graph is a better choice for showing trends, which is the primary purpose here.

Bar graphs

In Figure 8.3 you can compare the age demographics of different nursing programs, showing that, for example, associate

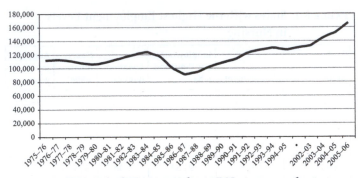

FIGURE 8.2 Annual admissions to basic RN programs, from
1975–76 to 1994–95 and 2002–03 to 2005–06.
Data were provided by the National League for Nursing, www.nln.org/research/
slides/index.htm.

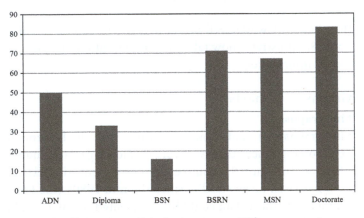

FIGURE 8.3 Percentage of students over age 30 by program type,
2012.
Data were provided by the National League for Nursing (2013), Annual Survey of
Schools of Nursing, Fall 2012, www.nln.org/research/slides/index.htm.

degree in nursing programs enroll a substantially larger percentage of students over thirty than baccalaureate degree programs. Bar graphs are usually the best choice for representing
comparisons.

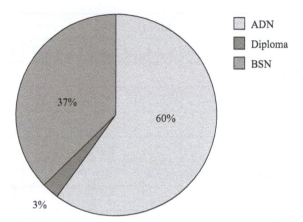

FIGURE 8.4 **RN graduation by program type, 2007–08.**
Data were provided by the National League for Nursing, www.nln.org/research/slides/index.htm.

Pie graphs
In Figure 8.4 you can see how nurses with associate degrees significantly dominate the recent nursing workforce. When you are trying to show the various *proportions* of elements that make up a whole, the pie chart is an apt choice. Avoid 3-D pie charts because they often visually distort those proportions.

Gantt charts
This style of chart was developed by Henry Gantt in the early twentieth century. Tasks (milestones) in a Gantt chart are arranged along the vertical axis in descending chronological sequence while the dates and durations of each task are shown along the horizontal axis (Figure 8.5).

Other charts or graphs that you might use in scientific, technical, or professional writing include the following.

	Months								
	1	2	3	4	5	6	7	8	9
Milestones									
Recruit participants	▓								
Intervention			▓		▓				
Data collection				▓		▓			
Data analysis							▓		
Poster presentation								▓	
Manuscript preparation								▓	
Publication									▓

FIGURE 8.5 Proposed health innovations research project timetable, showing recruitment, data collection and analysis, and dissemination.

Scatter graphs
Scatter graphs show correlations when data are variable. You might use this if you have gathered statistical data about a phenomenon.

Organizational charts
Organizational charts show the structure of an institution or entity. You might use this in a project concerning your nursing program or a health center.

Flow charts
Flow charts show a sequential process, including options and decisions. You might use this to show the different paths of the nursing process, including decisions about diagnosis, treatment, and evaluation.

How to avoid "chartjunk"

You might be tempted to "dress up" figures or tables, and design programs like Microsoft Word, PowerPoint, Excel, and Prezi provide you with a wide variety of colors, background shadings, 3-D renderings, animations, and the like. However, these embellishments usually add nothing to your analysis and can often make the table or figure more confusing or distracting. Academics typically see these as choosing style over substance, so more often than not, such visual embellishments hurt your credibility.

Maps

Maps show spatial relationships among data. You might use this in a project examining disease prevalence or health resources in a locale identified by ZIP codes or by states.

Photographs and Drawings

Photographs

Photographs show how something appears visually with details of shading or color. You might use this to represent a medical device or, in a color image, the manifestations of a disease. However, sometimes a photograph provides too many nuances of shading that obscure the crucial or essential elements (which is why airplane emergency procedure cards are drawn as cartoons).

Line and technical drawings

Line and technical drawings show objects in a clearer, simpler form without shading or color. You might use this to highlight a specific detail or a few details in a medical device.

Figure 8.6 shows a grayscale photograph of a hospital bedside call system. Although grayscale images accurately depict objects, their shading may provide too much detail or nuance that prevents your reader from seeing the main features. In Figure 8.7, a high-contrast line drawing of the grayscale photograph, you are able to show readers the main features more clearly, also bringing those features to readers' attention by the two callouts that point to and label the features.

Present Visuals in Consistent, Standard Formats

Simply plopping visuals into your text is a recipe for losing credibility with your audience. Academics prize precision and accuracy, and they demand that visuals meet certain

FIGURE 8.6 Hospital bedside call system.

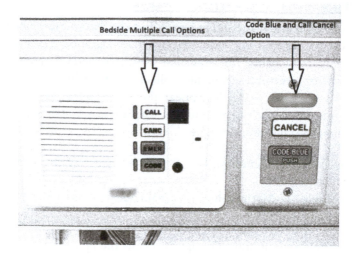

FIGURE 8.7 Hospital bedside call system, showing Call, Cancel, Emergency, and Code buttons, with the Code Blue system beside it; the unit includes a microphone and speaker for audio communication.

standards. Here are a few that are too commonly overlooked by students but always noticed by teachers and professionals.

Label

Give each visual a *label* with sequential Arabic numerals, numbered in the order in which they are mentioned in the text (e.g., Figure 1, Figure 2, Figure 3, or Table 1, Table 2, Table 3) rather than in the order in which they physically appear. In a work of multiple chapters (like the one you're reading now or a dissertation or procedure manual), figures and tables are numbered first with the chapter number followed by a decimal point and the sequential number of the figure or table (e.g., Figure 8.1, Figure 8.2, Figure 8.3 or Table 8.1, Table 8.2, Table 8.3).

Title

Give each visual a *title* that briefly and clearly describes what you are representing visually (e.g., "Demographic Data for Study Participants" [for a table] or "Research method timeline showing intervention and data collection" [for a figure]).

Table labels and titles appear above the tables. All major words begin with capital letters. Explanatory notes appear below the table. For example:

- Table 1. Demographic Characteristics of Research Participants
- Table 2. Methodological Characteristics of Literature Review Studies

Figure labels and titles appear below the figures; only the first words (and any proper nouns) are capitalized. Explanatory notes appear below the figure's label and title. For example:

- Figure 1. Disease incidence in three populations over 10 years. Data were provided by the Centers for Disease Control and Prevention.

Text

In the text of your writing, always explicitly refer the reader to tables and figures. For example:

- The study used a randomized sampling method that produced a sample whose demographic characters mirrored those of the population (see Table 1).
- See Figure 1 for a Gantt chart of project milestones, including intervention and data collection.

Better still, also use the text both immediately before your visual to prime your audience for how to receive it ("Notice how in the following graph . . .") and use the text immediately after to help your reader interpret it ("As this scatterplot reveals, there is a linear relationship between . . ."). Don't assume that a figure or table speaks for itself. You always need to explain to the reader the figure or table's significance.

Ethical Visual Representations

Misrepresenting data visually is as unethical as falsifying data in your text. For example, Figure 8.8 shows an accurate depiction of data, starting with zero as the baseline; the relationships are fairly and accurately represented in visual form. But in Figure 8.9, which represents the same data, the author has manipulated the visual depiction by starting at a baseline of ten, thus visually exaggerating the differences among the three values. If you are making graphs using software, such as Microsoft Excel, double-check the baseline—often the software gets it wrong.

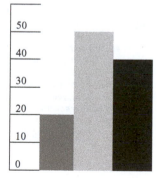

FIGURE 8.8 **Comparison of data.**

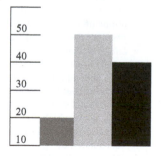

FIGURE 8.9 Comparison of data.

Effective Presentation Slides

You have no doubt sat through lectures or presentations (as have both of us) consisting of a series of PowerPoint slides that were dense with text, which the lecturer or presenter then proceeded to read to you (as if you couldn't read them yourself). While data and information are important, PowerPoint or Prezi visual presentations should be visual anchors, not a replication of the text of the presentation. Keep three simple guidelines in mind:

1. Use as few words or data points as possible on any one slide.
2. Provide visual impact with an effective and relevant image on as many slides as possible.
3. When possible, use charts and graphs to represent data.

Figures 8.10, 8.11, and 8.12 are from a presentation on sexual minority health based on a 2011 Institute of Medicine

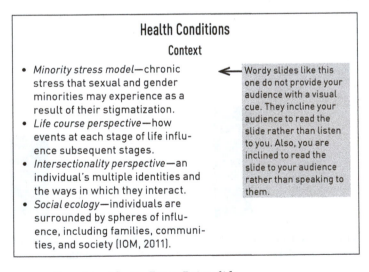

FIGURE 8.10 A text-heavy PowerPoint slide.

FIGURE 8.11   The same text as in Figure 8.10 with some visual variety with an image.

This slide is better. The addition of a figure provides your audience with a visual cue, but the problems noted above still pertain.

Finally, this slide provides a visual cue and brief verbal cues that orient the audience, which incline you to speak to rather than read to your audience.

FIGURE 8.12   A final revision of the slide showing the topic headings alone with the image.

report. They demonstrate an original text-heavy version, the same text with some visual variety with an image, and a final revision with the topic headings alone with the image.

Some presenters fill up their slides with text because they worry that they will forget what to say. If that describes you, use the Notes feature in PowerPoint (you see the notes but the audience doesn't) or write out your script separately. Keep your slides crisp and clean.

If providing detailed visuals, a densely populated table, or extended quotations is essential to your presentation, remember that distributing good old-fashioned hard copy handouts to your audience members can be an effective way to convey that information. They can consult the handouts as you speak.

Posters

A poster is a visual format rather than a genre. This format can be used to condense and present a variety of genres that we've discussed in previous chapters: a case study, a literature review, a research report, a clinical practice article. Either working alone or with a team of fellow nursing students, for example, you might be assigned to produce a poster on a clinical phenomenon. In their last semester of the senior year, our students at the University of Connecticut collaboratively prepare a practice improvement poster for their clinical capstone sites, presenting them at our annual on-campus research conference, which also features posters prepared by our honors students and graduate students collaborating with research faculty. Outstanding student posters might also be recommended for presentation at a conference, for which you would likely have to submit a proposal abstract (see Chapter 7).

If your proposal abstract has been accepted by the organizers of a conference, you will need to determine the precise poster format that the conference expects, including the dimensions (width, height) of the poster and its sections or headings. For example, the Eastern Nursing Research Society (ENRS) provides these guidelines for student poster presentations:

- ENRS will provide a numbered 4-foot (high) by 4-foot (wide) cork constructed board to post your presentation.
- Abstract title, author(s), and institution should be placed at the top of your poster board in large lettering. The abstract title should be about 1 inch high; authors and institution should be about 1 inch high.
- Your abstract will be listed in the ENRS 26th Annual Scientific Sessions Book of Proceedings; however, we also recommend that you post a large-type copy of your abstract in the upper left corner of your board so that attendees may easily refer to it.
- Please use large type size that can be easily read at a distance of 6 feet.
- Be sure graphs and charts can be easily read at a distance of 6 feet.
- All material should be printed on thin paper or poster paper. Keep in mind that a heavy board may be difficult to keep in place on the display.
- Materials may be mounted using pushpins, Velcro or thumbtacks.

ENRS also supplies the poster layout for nursing students. Visit the ENRS website (http://www.enrs-go.org/) for more information.

The University of Connecticut's School of Nursing provides the format shown in Figure 8.13 for its student and faculty posters.

FIGURE 8.13 Poster template (boxes for figures and tables are placeholders only).

TABLE 8.3 Typical Font Specifications for Conference Posters

Component	Type and Font Size
Title	Italic, 107 point
First author's name	Italic, 68 point
Second and subsequent authors' names	Italic, 43 point
Section headings	Roman bold, 48 point
Section text	Roman, 36 point
Figure and table labels and titles, and notes	Roman, 24 point

While this template provides you with a sense of the overall design of a poster, Table 8.3 specifies the font characteristics for each.

Beyond these technical specifications, step back and consider some broader design concerns:

- Most posters should be about 40 percent graphics, 30 percent text, and 30 percent white space. Note the importance of white space, especially around the borders and around the text and images. Such space is important to allow the eye to rest.
- Follow the guidelines outlined earlier in this chapter when making strategic decisions about what kinds of figures to include in your poster.
- Make color matter. In general, cool colors (blues, greens) work better than warm ones (red, orange, yellow), and high contrast is important. Avoid a color background; it not only adds unnecessary printing cost but also creates distraction in neutral white space.
- Create an intuitive reading path. The templates do much of this for you, but test how your eye travels—where it starts, where it goes next, where it pauses.
- Make sure you can communicate your research as a story. Be prepared with a quick initial pitch about your research— one you are likely to repeat many times—as people come up to browse your poster.

USAGE AND STYLE

In this chapter we outline some of the common usage and style problems that writers encounter and offer helpful guidelines. We cannot cover everything, so instead we have selected items that we see most often in our teaching and editing; we also consulted colleagues in the University of Connecticut's School of Nursing and members of the International Academy of Nurse Editors. If you attend carefully to these editing details, you will earn more credibility with your readers, which inclines them to care more about your writing. Conversely, if you are not careful enough in your editing, readers may question both your competence and credibility.

A quick note about process: many professional writers do not obsess about sentence-level matters every time they sit down to compose, and some even dash off sloppy early drafts. They understand that obsessing too much about grammar, usage, and style too early in the writing process can lead to painfully slow writing, writer's block, or stilted prose. Yet those same professional writers know that the freedom they give themselves in early generative stages of composing must be matched with an equal commitment late in the writing process to editing and proofreading. In both cases, this means that you are not working on a paper at the last minute before a deadline!

What do we mean by *usage*? Language is a living practice that undergoes change continuously. How we use phrases and clauses in sentences, how we use words, and how we use punctuation are all subject to change. We think of language less in terms of "correctness" or "errors" than in terms of current *standard* and *nonstandard* usage. When enough academic and professional writers employ a new usage, the usage becomes standard. Indeed, in later editions of this book, we may have to update our advice because professional usage over time changes the standard.

What do we mean by *style*? In the context of academic writing, *style* has many (often competing) denotations. It can mean a distinctive way of assembling sentences and paragraphs that allows the alert reader to recognize who the author is without seeing the author's name. In other words, you recognize the writing *voice* of the author. It can also mean your adherence to a set of conventions for formatting your academic writing and citing its sources. In that sense we speak of academic writers using *American Psychological Association (APA) style* (the most common style sheet in nursing's academic writing) or *American Medical Association (AMA) style* (used by some nurses but more common among physicians and other medical writers). However, we have a middle sense in mind: the learned craft of techniques whereby you assemble words into clear sentences, sentences into coherent paragraphs, and paragraphs into cogent explanations or arguments.

Common Grammar Usage Issues

Noun/Verb Consistency

Verbs are forms of words that convey physical action (e.g., The nurse *collected* blood samples), mental activity (e.g., The researcher *hypothesizes* a counter-intuitive result), or states of being (e.g., The nursing staff *were* puzzled by the response).

Verb forms need to be consistent with the noun or pronoun that serves as the sentence's subject according to whether that subject is singular or plural (e.g., The researcher [singular] *hypothesizes*; The researchers [plural] *hypothesize*). Writers sometimes get into trouble with noun/verb consistency when the subject and verb are not close to each other:

- *Inconsistent*: The clinician and researcher [plural compound subject], each one contributing her expertise to the project, was [singular] aware of the limitation. (Here the insertion of the phrase starting with *each* and featuring the two singular nouns *expertise* and *project* resulted in the writer getting lost.)
- *Consistent*: The clinician and researcher [plural compound subject], each one contributing her expertise to the project, were [plural] aware of the limitation.

Noun/Pronoun Consistency

Nouns are forms of words that name a person, place, thing, quality, or activity. Pronouns are words that replace a noun. As such, a pronoun must agree with the noun it replaces in *number* (singular or plural) and *gender* (masculine, feminine, neuter [i.e., can be used for men, women, or both]).

- *Consistent*: When Nurse Mildred Ratched [singular female, proper noun] dispensed medications to her [feminine possessive pronoun] patients, she [feminine pronoun] did so in a regimented fashion. The other nurses [plural noun] however, resented that they [neuter plural pronoun] were not able to dispense medications to their [neuter plural possessive pronoun] patients.

Sentences like that one come fairly naturally to native speakers of English, but one thing that trips up many writers is using "they" when referring back to a singular noun. In speech, this sounds natural and is often used to render gender-neutral language, but in writing it violates noun/pronoun consistency:

- *Inconsistent*: When a nurse [singular] begins a shift, they [plural] need to remember to wash their [plural] hands.

  For which standard usage would be:

- *Consistent*: When a nurse [singular] begins a shift, he or she [singular] needs to remember to wash his or her [singular] hands.

While this is technically correct and attempts to be gender inclusive, it is also clumsy. So a better solution, where possible, is to convert both the noun and pronouns to plural:

- *Consistent*: When nurses [plural] begin a shift, they [plural] need to remember to wash their [plural] hands.

However, having said that, usage does change over time, and with increasing frequency we observe that the shift from a singular noun (*a nurse*) to a neuter plural pronoun (*they*) has become acceptable professional usage in many settings.

Vague Pronoun Reference

This occurs most frequently with the pronouns "it" or "they." When pronouns appear in a sentence but have no clear antecedent—or when one pronoun could refer to more than one antecedent—this irks academic readers because they prize precision and clarity.

- *Vague*: All health care workers are told repeatedly that handwashing is effective in preventing the spread of infection.

They [Who is "they"? Not the "health care workers" of the previous sentence!] emphasize *it* [What specifically does this refer back to?] through training and signage, but many still do not follow *it* [Another unclear antecedent] regularly.

- *Clear*: All health care workers are told repeatedly that washing hands is effective in preventing the spread of infection. *Managers* promote *that rule* through training and signage, but many clinicians still do not follow *it* [This is OK now because it clearly refers to "that rule"] regularly.

- *Clear*: Managers repeatedly tell health care workers that *they* [OK because it clearly refers to "workers"] should wash *their* hands to prevent the spread of infection. Despite all that training and signage, many workers still do not follow *those rules* [Cannot use "it" here because the antecedent wouldn't exist]. [This revised version employs the active voice, which we discuss in a later section of this chapter.]

Who/Whom

Students *who* are confused about these two words often feel that there is no one to *whom* they can turn for help. *Who* is the nominative or subject form of the pronoun while *whom* is the objective or object form. Is the pronoun acting as the subject or actor? (*Who* is asking this question?) Is the pronoun acting as the object of the clause or object of a preposition—that is, is being acted upon? (You may be unclear *whom* you should ask about this usage, but the professor from *whom* you are taking this course can help you.) When in doubt, stick with *who*.

Plurals and Possessives

English nouns have a quality known as *number* (they are singular or plural), and typically they distinguish a plural noun by adding *-s* or *-es*. You do not signal that a noun is plural by using an apostrophe (*'s* or *s'*); an apostrophe is used to distinguish possessive nouns. Also note that some English nouns are un-countable, such as *evidence* and *research,* and thus are never pluralized. See the discussion below of punctuation and apostrophes for more information on punctuating possessives.

Common Word Usage Issues

Regardless/irrespective. Do not use "irregardless."

> *Regardless* of how much it will cost our health center, we provide the same quality of care to all patients *irrespective* of their ability to pay.

You're/your. You're is a contraction of the phrase *you are; your* is a personal possessive pronoun.

> In *your* first full-time job as a nurse, *you're* [you are] likely to find that some of *your* clinical institution's practices are not evidence based.

They're/there/their. They're is a contraction of the phrase *they are; there* is a demonstrative pronoun; *their* is a plural personal possessive pronoun.

> When new nurses start their first full-time jobs, *they're* [they are] likely to find that some veteran nurses who have been *there* a long time are set in *their* ways.

It's/its. It's is a contraction of the phrase *it is; its* is a singular possessive pronoun.

> *It's* [it is] a common belief that a clinic is only as good as *its* care of *its* most vulnerable patients.

Toward. Do not use "towards."

In forming a task force that included housekeeping, cleri-cal, nursing, and medical staff, the hospital was moving *toward* a total quality model of improvement.

Based on. Do not use "based off of."

Our health center undertook these changes in admission procedures *based on* the data we collected from anony-mous surveys and focus groups.

Impact is a noun. Many now use it as a verb, but most editors prefer that instead you use *affect* [to have an effect or to cause an impact upon someone or something, or to touch someone emotionally].

The director of nursing was not certain how these changes would *affect* [verb] the morale of the nursing staff, but the evidence of a healthy *impact* [noun] on patients was compelling.

Famous is a good thing. "Notorious" and "infamous" are not.

The *famous* 1948 Declaration of Geneva (the World Medical Association's physician's oath) was prepared partly in re-sponse to the *infamous* medical "experiments" conducted by *notorious* Nazi physicians in concentration camps.

Use can be a verb or noun. In nearly all cases, it is better to employ the simpler and more accurate *use* than to puff up your language with "utilize" or "utilization."

In that study the researchers *used* [a verb] a randomized controlled trial of the new therapy. In their *use* [a noun] of the protocol they followed ethical standards and sound science.

Since/because/thus/as. "Since" and "as" imply that some time has passed. On almost every occasion requiring cause-and-effect analysis, "because" or "thus" is a better choice.

Since [i.e., *after*] we instituted the new infection control protocols nine months ago, our infection rates have steadily declined, *because* all employees understand that they are part of the solution. *As* [when] new employees join us, we provide training, *thus* requiring a more robust residency program.

Which vs. that. This distinction is disappearing, but it deserves some explanation. *Which* and *that* are relative pronouns that introduce dependent clauses adding some clarification to the main clause of a sentence. Traditionally, if the clarifying clause is a restrictive clause (you need to have it to make sense), then *that* is used; if the clarifying clause is unrestrictive (it adds information but the sentence makes sense without it), *which* is used.

The HIPAA-compliance continuing education, *which* will cost our health center $23,000, addresses a federal mandate *that* requires all health organizations to provide training *that* informs employees of privacy requirements. (Notice that the non-restrictive clause [the sentence would make sense if you were to delete the clause] is separated by commas while the restrictive clause [the sentence wouldn't make sense if you were to delete it] is not separated.)

Who/that. Relative pronouns refer back to people [*who*] or things [*that*] previously mentioned in the sentence. Do not use "that" for people.

> Nursing students *who* performed poorly in anatomy and physiology courses may struggle in their advanced clinical science courses. Nursing programs *that* are designed for student success will provide supplementary education.

Affect/effect. Affect is a verb meaning to influence, act on, work on, have an impact on, or touch emotionally; *effect* is usually employed as a noun, but it can also be used as a verb that means to cause something to happen, and is usually phrased as "to effect change."

> Although the nursing team was not able to *effect* the changes that they proposed, their efforts alerted their colleagues to the problem and positively *affected* their practices.

Great/huge/tons of and other hyperboles. Avoid vague words, especially words designed to emphasize scale or size. A more technically standard word is *significant* or *significantly* or *considerable* or *substantial.*

> Public health nurses working in clinics have reported *significant* [rather than *huge*] increases in sexually transmitted diseases, which suggests that HIV infection rates might also increase *significantly.* There are *considerable* data and *substantial* [rather than *tons of*] evidence to warrant concern. (This is the general usage, but in statistics, *significant* has a different, more technical meaning.)

Increased/decreased. Use these instead of "went up" or "went down."

> The researchers observed that infection rates *decreased* during the education program's three years of operation and *increased* after the grant for the program ended.

Data are/data show. The word *data* is a plural noun, so it requires a plural verb.

> These *data are* a reliable proxy for other quality measures. The *data show* that nurses have a positive influence on reducing the time that a patient has to stay in the hospital. (The singular form of *data* is *datum,* which is used rarely because most nursing science relies on an accumulation of data.)

Here/hear. The first is an adverb that indicates location; the second is a verb meaning *to listen to.*

> If you place the stethoscope *here,* you can listen to the heartbeat more accurately and *hear* any irregularities.

Than/then. The first is a conjunction used in comparisons; the second is usually an adverb to indicate a sequence of time.

> If the patient's body temperature rises higher *than* 101 degrees Fahrenheit, *then* you should consider fever-reducing measures.

Versus means "opposed to" or "in conflict with"; do not use *vice* or *verse* (the phrase *vice versa* means "the opposite" or "the other way around").

Words ending in –st. Novice writers sometimes forget that plural forms of nouns ending in *–st* must have the letter *s* added, just as you would with noun.

> The surgical department's *anesthesiologists* were impressed with the credentials and skill of the newly hired nurse *anesthetist.*

Subjects, participants, and populations. Novice writers sometimes get into trouble when referring to populations or groups of patients. Historically, patients or others who participate in research projects have been called *research subjects.* More recently, however, researchers concerned about the ethical treatment of patients or others and committed to seeing them as more than passive subjects upon whom instruments and treatments are administered have taken to referring to them as *research participants.* When referring generically to a patient group, the word *population* is usually used. Technical names for gender, sexual, racial, and ethnic identities also deserve special attention. The terms *gender identity* and *sexual orientation* are now standard (rather than *sexual preference*), as are *transgender person, lesbians, gay men* (rather than *homosexual*), *bisexual men,* and *bisexual women.* For racial and ethnic identities, the terms *Black* or *African American, White, Asian American, Native American* or *American Indian* or *Native North American,* and *Hispanic* or *Latino* or *Chicano* (depending on where a person is from) are standard. They are all capitalized as proper nouns.

Punctuation

In Chapter 10 we explain how punctuation is used in quoting and citing sources in APA style, but here we want to alert you to a few punctuation problems we see too often.

Colons

Everyone uses periods and commas but not enough students make use of the colon, which functions to introduce a series of items, an emphatic statement, or long block quotation.

- Nurse Ratched had three requests: more structured activity time for patients, increased staff, and greater autonomy in dispensing medication.
- Major Margaret Houlihan, RN, was insistent when she met with the chief of surgery: she would request a transfer if conditions did not improve.

Semicolons

These join sentences (i.e., independent clauses) that could each stand alone but that are related in such a way that they can be effectively combined into a single sentence.

- Catherine Barkley, RN, was shocked to find that the supply room was in a disordered state; she began to remedy it immediately.

Apostrophes

The single apostrophe is used in two circumstances: to indicate a word contraction (i.e., the combining of two words) or a signal that a noun is possessive. For example: *can't* is a contraction of *cannot*; *it's* is a contraction of *it is*; *won't* is a contraction of *will not*. Some professors, editors, and other readers view contractions as informal or colloquial, so you might consider avoiding contractions in formal writing. (Notice that we've honored that principle more in the breach than in the observance throughout this book!) Apostrophes are also used to show that a noun is possessive.

- This *nurse's* dilemma demonstrates the need to expand all *nurses'* scope of practice. (In the first instance, a singular noun is made possessive by the addition of *'s*, while in the second, a plural noun already ending in *s* is shown as possessive by adding the apostrophe at the end of the word [*s'*].)

Apostrophes are **never** used to signal plural number:

- *Incorrect*: Almost 100 *nurse's* responded to the survey.
- *Correct*: Almost 100 *nurses* responded to the survey

Quotation Marks

Sometimes called single apostrophes (in British punctuation) and double apostrophes (in American punctuation), these marks are used to identify verbatim quotations. They are also sometimes used to identify publication titles. In most cases in American writing, the double quotation mark is used. If your original source is using a quotation, however, you will place that quotation in single quotation marks and the entire source that you are quoting in double quotation marks. For example, if your source says:

Among the respondents there were a variety of responses, but many poignantly echoed this respondent, "I'd come to the end of the road and couldn't see any remedy."

You would quote the source this way:

As Baylor (2013) observes, "Among the respondents there were a variety of responses, but many poignantly echoed this respondent, 'I'd come to the end of the road and couldn't see any remedy'" (p. 23).

This is known as a quote within a quote. One final point concerning quotation marks: do not use quotation marks to call attention to a word or to "emphasize" it; instead *italicize* the word.

Capitalization

Capitalization rules vary according to the style manual that you are using. The APA *Publication Manual* (2010, pp. 101–104) provides the following guidelines for capitalization:

- Words beginning a sentence
- Major words in titles and headings (but not definite or indefinite articles *the* and *a/an*, short prepositions, and conjunctions)
- Proper nouns and trade names
- Nouns followed by numbers (e.g., "on Day 3 of Intervention 2")
- Official titles of tests or instruments

Acronyms and Abbreviations

Abbreviations are commonly used in nursing research writing, and the APA *Publications Manual* (2010, pp. 106–111, 117–123) provides guidelines for their use.

When using an abbreviation as a shorthand device, in the first instance provide the full phrase followed by the abbreviation in parentheses. Use only the abbreviation thereafter.

Researchers administered the Postpartum Depression Screening Scale (PDSS) to all of the study's participants. [Thereafter you will simply refer to the instrument as the PDSS.]

Some abbreviations are commonly accepted as words and require no explanation (e.g., IQ, HIV, AIDS, RN).

Use *Merriam-Webster's Collegiate Dictionary* as the arbiter of such words.

Abbreviations for Latin words and phrases are common: e.g. ("for example"), i.e. ("that is"), etc. ("and so forth"), et al. ("and all the others"), vs. ("versus" or "against").

Scientific abbreviations, particularly for measurements, appear commonly in health literature: cm (centimeter), dl (deciliter), °F (degrees Fahrenheit), g (gram), IU (international unit), L (liter), mg (milligram), mmHg (millimeters of mercury).

Finally, abbreviations are used for a variety of statistical terms frequently employed in quantitative studies: ANOVA (analysis of variance), M (mean or average), Mdn (median), N (total number of cases), n (number of a subset of the total number of cases).

Style

As we pointed out in the introduction to this chapter, style is about more than grammar. Here are a few tips to apply as you write and revise for an effective style.

Active/Passive Voice

Active voice entails a clause in which the subject (the doer of an action) precedes the *verb* (the action), which is then followed by the object of the action. In the active voice the doer of an action is clear and is followed by the verb for the *action*, which is followed by the object of the action. For example:

> *Active voice*: The clinical nurses [doer] collected [action] the blood samples [object], the lab technicians conducted the assays of the blood samples, and the researcher performed the data analysis.

In the *passive voice* these relationships are turned around: the object precedes the verb and the doer of the action is merely implied. A fairly reliable indicator of the passive voice is the use of "to be" verbs (e.g., is, am, be, was, and were), but sentences can still be in passive voice even without those verbs.

> *Passive voice*: The blood samples [object] were collected [verb], the assays were conducted, and the data analysis was performed.

The *APA Publication Manual* (2010, p. 77) advises you to use the active voice because, although many students *think* passive sentences sound smarter, most readers find passive sentences harder to comprehend. (For example, here's that last sentence recast in the passive: "The passive voice is preferred by many students because it is assumed by them that it makes them sound smarter, but the resulting sentences actually result in increased comprehension difficulty." Much worse, right?) There is even an ethical dimension to the active/passive question. For example, the passive voice "Mistakes were made" hides the doer/agent, which most readers consider evasive, perhaps even irresponsible; the active voice, on the other hand, makes agents own their actions. One common revision exercise involves underlining all the "to be" verbs in a draft and then trying to convert as many of them as you can to the active voice. However, the APA's *Manual* observes that there are situations when it is appropriate to use the passive—for example, when you wish to emphasize *how* the research activities were performed (rather than *who* performed them).

Concision

Many of us write wordy early drafts. This is alright, but it obliges us to ruthlessly prune all unnecessary words from our final draft. Readers appreciate economical prose.

- *Wordy*: Due to the fact that some writers think that the length of a sentence is an indicator of just how smart you are and how intelligent it sounds, principles of concision can very often be ignored in favor of sentences that are long in size. Also, some additional writers insert additional words in sentences in a desperate ploy for the purpose of meeting a page expectation for an academic paper in a course.
- *Concise*: Because many writers think long sentences sound smart, they ignore principles of concision. Others insert extra words in a desperate ploy to meet the page expectations for their academic papers.

Many phrases in the first passage are filler and can simply be cut; several others are repetitious or implied (smart ~~and intelligent~~; long ~~in size~~). Notice also how converting the sentences to active voice helps with both concision and comprehension.

When possible, trade phrases for single words (*Due to the fact that = Because*). Apply that same principle to introductory phrases, such as *It was/there was/there were,* which can often be cut entirely:

- *Wordy*: It was a nurse who discovered the medication error.
- *Concise*: A nurse discovered the medication error.

Parallelism

While the first sentence below is not grammatically wrong, it is stylistically careless because the third item in the list breaks grammatical parallelism (improved in the second sentence).

- *Not parallel*: Nursing writers usually succeed by <u>understanding</u> the health care organizations they work for, <u>mastering</u> a set of genre conventions, and <u>they must be open to learning from those around them.</u>

- *Parallel*: Nursing writers usually succeed by <u>understanding</u> the health care organizations they work for, <u>mastering</u> a set of genre conventions, and <u>maintaining</u> an attitude that is open to learning.

For another example, see the first sentence under the *Colon* heading earlier in this chapter. The principle of parallelism applies not just to sentences but also to bulleted lists. Even in your PowerPoint and poster presentations, items in bulleted lists should be as parallel in syntax as possible.

Paragraphs and Transitions

Unity and focus, coherence and sequence, length: like a room in a house, the paragraph is part of a larger structure and one whose careful design will make it clear and effective. Think about a well-designed and well-equipped kitchen. There's a place for everything, and everything's in its place. It's an efficient place to work, without clutter. Paragraphs work the same way. Paragraphs should usually begin with a *topic sentence* that signals to the reader the new idea to which you are turning. Each sentence should then follow in a coherently linear sequence, taking readers step by step through a process or argument. Paragraphs should end with a concluding sentence that summarizes the main point of the paragraph or points to the next paragraph. In previous chapters we have provided you with examples of writing in a variety of genres, noting how the style of writing is different in each of them. An example from one of our students shows how attention to a few details enhances paragraph unity and coherence:

> Lack of support from health care providers is one of the most significant predictors of emotional and personal strain, role overload, and role captivity among caregivers of community-dwelling patients with dementia. Caregivers

of patients with Alzheimer's disease are **also** significantly more likely to require bereavement services after patient death than other diagnoses, and if not receiving hospice care, these bereavement needs are usually left unsupported. **Moreover**, nearly half of caregivers showed clinically significant levels of depression during the last few months of the patient's life, which is higher than rates of depression among caregivers of other diseases. Lower level of satisfaction with social supports is significantly also associated with post-loss depression among caregivers. **Finally**, caregiver burden is one of the top two reasons for institutionalization of patients with dementia, which is associated with lower quality of life for the patient.

The first sentence signals the paragraph's central theme (a topic sentence). The highlighted transitional words (*also, moreover, finally*) guide readers through the sequence from one idea to the next. Indeed, sophisticated writers use such transitions— sometimes called *linking words* or *signposts*—precisely and purposefully. They also introduce variety in their use of transitions.

- *To add to an idea or show similarity*: furthermore, also, and, besides, moreover, next, in addition, further, first, second, third
- *To draw contrast, reveal counter-arguments, or show reservations*: in contrast, but, however, on the contrary, conversely, nonetheless, otherwise, yet, on the other hand
- *To introduce an example*: for example, for instance, in particular
- *To clarify*: in other words, that is, to clarify
- *To signal cause and effect*: because, for that reason, on account of, since, accordingly, as a result, consequently, hence, therefore, thus

- *To conclude*: finally, in conclusion, in short, in summary, to conclude

Inappropriate Metonymy and Personification

Metonymy is the technical term for substituting one thing for another closely related thing. For example, an advertisement reads, "Hospitals trust Tylenol," but hospitals are inanimate and can't trust (or mistrust) anything. Rather, the professional people inside (nurses, doctors) might trust the efficacy and safety of a medication, and your writing should reflect that reality ("Hospital nurses and physicians trust Tylenol"). Another common example of this error is "The *study* examined this phenomenon." But studies are inanimate, so better phrasing would be "The *researchers* examined this phenomenon." Studies don't examine anything; people do.

Avoid "I Think That/I Believe That"

Readers assume that when you make a statement of interpretation or opinion, it is what you think or believe. Occasionally these phrases are OK if you are intentionally trying to *hedge*— that is, trying soften your claims or signal a lower degree of confidence in your claim (which is sometimes a fitting move).

Avoid Editorializing and Grandstanding

Nurses' academic and professional writing employs an objective and dispassionate tone, even when it is explaining or making an argument about a controversial or serious issue. It allows the power of facts and the strength of an argument to persuade the readers, rather than hyperventilating language. When you find your writing sounding like a speech by a preacher or politician, it's time to dial it back.

SYNTHESIZING AND CITING SOURCES

In this final chapter we reprise a theme we've woven throughout but apply it to working with sources. Only by synthesizing and citing sources can you solidify your *credibility* as a nurse researcher, persuade your readers to *care* about your topic, and show your *competence* as an informed clinician. In Chapter 2, we showed you how to observe a clinical phenomenon and to search and evaluate the research literature in order to understand the phenomenon. In Chapters 3 through 7 we explained how to use the research literature and other evidence in clinical, academic, and professional writing. In this chapter we explain how to summarize and synthesize sources, and how to cite them with parenthetical in-text citations and references using American Psychological Association (APA) style.

How to Summarize and Paraphrase

In some academic writing or college composition settings you are taught how to integrate quotations elegantly or seamlessly into a paper. However, in the health sciences like nursing, direct quotations are rarely used. Instead, authors summarize (distill and condense a source in their own words) or paraphrase (represent a specific passage from a source in their own words). Summarizing and paraphrasing demonstrate your mastery of the material.

There are three steps in the process of summarizing or paraphrasing: read, condense, and represent.

1. *Read*: Read the abstract (if it is a journal article) or the introduction (if it is a book or book chapter). Skim the journal article, paying attention to its headings and sub-headings, or skim the table of contents if it is a book. Then, carefully read the journal article, book chapter, or book, taking notes while you do so. Pay careful attention to the topic sentences of paragraphs (usually the first sentence), which often identify the main ideas within each paragraph.
2. *Condense*: Put the article or book chapter aside. Review your notes. Outline the main ideas or key points using bulleted lists or complete sentences. Check it for accuracy by reviewing the original source.
3. *Represent*: Write a summary or paraphrase of the relevant material from your notes, outlines, and memory.

When you summarize, you condense a larger body of ideas and information into far fewer words. You should be able to summarize an entire article in one or two sentences (though you may also use a full paragraph to do so). You should be able to summarize a book in a single paragraph.

When you paraphrase, you take a source's ideas and information and present them in your own language. Typically, in a paraphrase you use less formal or less technical language than you find in the original source. Paraphrasing does *not* involve changing just a few words of the original source; instead, you must paraphrase passages in your own language, in syntax that departs from the original, and in a style appropriate to the audience and purpose of the document you are working on.

Students often struggle with determining when they have sufficiently paraphrased. Here we illustrate a poor attempt at paraphrase followed by a more skilled paraphrase. For this example, we use as the original source the American Nurses Association (ANA) policy statement on assisted suicide:

Original source: Nurses have an opportunity to create environments where patients feel comfortable to express thoughts, feelings, conflict, and despair. The issues that surround a request for assisted suicide should be explored with the patient, and as appropriate with family and team members. It is crucial to listen to and acknowledge the patient's expressions of suffering, hopelessness, and sadness. Factors that contribute to such a request should be further assessed and a plan of care initiated to address the patient's physical and emotional needs. Discussion of suicidal thoughts does not increase the risk of suicide and may actually be therapeutic in decreasing the likelihood. The relationship and communication between the nurse and patient can diminish feelings of isolation and provide needed support. (ANA, 2013)

A weak paraphrase only changes a few words and is actually considered a form of plagiarism. The few changes that the student made from the original are in bold face:

Weak paraphrase: Nurses **can** create environments where patients feel comfortable **expressing** thoughts, feelings, conflict, and despair. A request for assisted suicide should be explored with the patient, **as well as** family and team members. **Nurses should** listen to and acknowledge the patient's expressions of suffering, hopelessness, and sadness.

Factors **contributing** to such a request should be further assessed and a plan of care initiated to address the patient's physical and emotional needs. **Expressing** suicidal thoughts does not increase the risk of suicide and may actually be therapeutic in decreasing the likelihood. The relationship and communication between the nurse and patient can **reduce** feelings of isolation and provide needed support (ANA, 2013).

A more skilled paraphrase absorbs the main ideas from the source, which the writer expresses primarily in his or her own words. Notice that both the language and the syntax are transformed:

Skilled paraphrase: The American Nurses Association recognizes the important role that nurses have at the end of life when patients may be despondent about their prognosis. Encouraging patients to express their feelings is an important part of the nurse's role, and giving patients permission to be open about their desire to die does not increase the likelihood that they will take their own lives. When patients express a desire to end their lives, and even to request assistance in committing suicide, nurses should be willing to talk with them about this desire and the reasons for it. Attention to patients' holistic needs, including emotional as well as physical needs, is part of nursing practice (ANA, 2013).

By effectively paraphrasing material from an external source, you also shape the emphasis of the source to suit the purpose and audience of your current writing.

How to Position Sources into Your Explanation or Argument

Fashioning arguments with, through, or against these sources demonstrates your credibility by showing that you understand the state of knowledge, that your argument is credible, and that you use the evidence to support your position. By using sources in an argument you are entering into an ongoing conversation about your topic. While there are many well-established options from which you can choose when crafting your own argument, we think that the four most commonly used options in nursing writing are these.

Summarize What the Sources Say

For example, Cheryl Beck summarizes in four sentences the central idea of a twenty-three-page article describing the concept of posttraumatic growth:

> Calhoun and Tedeschi (1998) used the metaphor of an earthquake to illustrate posttraumatic growth. When a person experiences a traumatic event, the groundwork is laid for the potential of posttraumatic growth. Key to this development may be the traumatic event's ability to shake the base of the person's assumptions about the world. The traumatic experience needs to be strong enough, like an earthquake, to achieve this severe shaking of a person's understanding of the world.

Summarize the Consensus View

This summary might be simply condensed in a sentence or two:

> Research has confirmed the negative effects that postpartum depression has on mother–infant interactions and on the children's cognitive and emotional development.

Disagree with Sources or the Consensus While Explaining Your Disagreement

For example, as Cheryl has written:

> There are two common assumptions about qualitative research that can harm a program of research. The first assumption is that qualitative research is a jumping-off point in a research program that is followed by quantitative research studies, and the second is that qualitative methods should only be used with a topic area where not much is known or until hypotheses are ready to be tested. Both of these assumptions are based on the mistaken notion that qualitative research is not as rigorous or as valuable as quantitative research.

Acknowledge Others' Objections or Make Concessions to Objections While Still Holding Fast to Your View

For example, in an op-ed essay in the *Hartford Courant*, published when the Connecticut legislature was considering a bill to expand APRNs' scope of practice, Cusson and Alexander (2014) wrote:

> Some critics claim that an expanded role for APRNs would undermine the team approach that is reasonably seen as the pathway out of our expensive but not uniformly effective health care. They fret that the expanded role for APRNs is an untested novelty. They warn that fully autonomous APRNs would inhibit coordination of patient care. There are, however, already a variety of roles that APRNs perform today.

Integrating Sources into Your Writing

One of the challenges facing you as a novice writer is how to integrate sources in a way that is stylistically smooth and engaging while also clear and effective. There are several basic ways of doing this: *summarizing* the argument of an entire book or journal article in a condensed form (usually one or two sentences); *paraphrasing* another author's material in your own words; using a *short-excerpt verbatim quotation,* placed within question marks; and using a *longer verbatim quotation* (forty or more words), placed within a block indent format. You can either introduce the names of your sources within a sentence or reserve the citation for the end of the sentence.

In this section, we are using a book that one of us (Tom Long) wrote, which argues that during the worst years of the HIV/AIDS epidemic in the United States (the decade and a half before the introduction of antiretroviral treatments), American public discourse about AIDS was dominated by apocalyptic or end-of-the-world rhetoric used by both religious conservatives and AIDS activists (Long, 2005).

Summarizing the book might look like this:

> According to Long (2005) public debates about HIV/ AIDS were dominated by apocalyptic rhetoric that was effective in marshaling attention and alarm but not a useful strategy for long-term chronic disease management.

or

> During the first decade and a half of the AIDS epidemic both religious conservatives and AIDS activists used apocalyptic rhetoric in ways that were effective in mobilizing action but not useful in the hard work of disease management (Long, 2005).

You cite the source at the front end (top example) or back end (bottom example) of the sentence, but not in both places.

Paraphrasing a paragraph in the book might look like this:

During the first decade and a half of the HIV/AIDS epidemic different social groups struggled for representational power within competing cultural systems. Christian fundamentalists, sex radicals, and AIDS activists alike employed apocalyptic rhetoric, using this language for their own aims (Long, 2005, p. 2).

Notice that here you need to include the page number of the passage you paraphrased because it comes from a book.

Short-excerpt verbatim quotations (under forty words, placed in quotation marks) might be integrated into your own writing:

According to Long (2005), apocalyptic rhetoric surrounding the AIDS epidemic appeared "not only among Christian fundamentalists but also within groups most affected by AIDS" (p. 2). In addition, AIDS activists and artists affected by AIDS "attempted to wrest control of hostile apocalyptic images by appropriating the texts for their own purposes" (Long, 2005, p. 2).

Notice that the quotations are integrated or woven into the author's own writing rather than simply dropped in as full sentences.

Longer verbatim quotations (over forty words, placed in block quotation) might be inserted if their ideas or ideas are particularly effective:

As one cultural study has observed:

During the first AIDS decade, the coincidence of male homosexuality with a hideously fatal infectious agent intensified this apocalyptic rhetoric, not only among

Christian fundamentalists but also within those groups most affected by AIDS. Through the 1980s and into the second decade of the epidemic, HIV/AIDS-affected/infected culture workers attempted to wrest control of hostile apocalyptic images by appropriating them for their own purposes. That two opposed groups in American cultural politics could each employ the same tropes for competing ideological purposes attests both to the pervasiveness of apocalypticism in American culture and to the resilience of its signs. (Long, 2005, p. 2)

Thus the AIDS epidemic presented a paradoxical use of the same kinds of rhetoric for quite different purposes.

Notice that the block quotation does not include quotation marks (the block indent signals that it is a quotation) and that the quotation is introduced by a signal phrase (*As one cultural study has observed:*).

We should point out that APA style prefers *summarizing* and *paraphrasing* instead of using verbatim quotations. Summarizing and paraphrasing demonstrate the extent to which you have made another's ideas your own. Novice writers who rely on verbatim quotations often end up with a patchwork quilt of quotations, with half their paper written by somebody else! A good rule of thumb for deciding whether to use a quotation is to ask yourself: *Is the other person's wording or phrasing so exact, so eloquent, and so indispensable that clarity and impact would be lost if I paraphrased it?*

Let's take a look at some examples to see how student writers typically employ citations and quotations. We will point out the strengths and weaknesses in students' use of sources. The first comes from a student's paper entitled "Obese

Women's Perceptions and Experiences of Healthcare and Primary Care Providers: A Critique," which evaluates a research article. In an introductory paragraph the student wrote:

> The research problem is the rate of obesity, which Buxton and Snethen (2013) support by supplementing the article with research studies showing that prevalence rates of obesity in adults have been increasing over the past 25 years. "Yet new data suggest that the rates of obesity appear to be leveling off (Flegal, Carroll, Kit, & Ogden, 2012)" (as cited in Buxton & Snethen, 2013, p. 252). Using a phenomenological qualitative tradition is a good fit for this study because the patients are providing in-depth meaning and essence through lived experiences.

Notice that the student has correctly written *Buxton and Snethen* when the authors' names appear in the sentence and *Buxton & Snethen* when their names appear in the in-text parenthetical citation. The citations are correct. However, the student simply drops the quotation in between two of her own sentences without using signal words or phrases. We would suggest the following revision:

> The research problem is the rate of obesity, which Buxton and Snethen (2013) support by supplementing the article with research studies showing that prevalence rates of obesity in adults have been increasing over the past 25 years. They point out, however, that "new data suggest that the rates of obesity appear to be leveling off (Flegal, Carroll, Kit, & Ogden, 2012)" (Buxton & Snethen, 2013, p. 252). Using a phenomenological qualitative tradition is a good fit for this study because the patients are providing in-depth meaning and essence through lived experiences.

Another student writing a critique of the same article effectively integrates a quotation from the secondary literature (*Essentials of Nursing Research: Appraising Evidence for Nursing Practice*, a 2014 textbook by Polit and Beck) as well as the primary source (Buxton and Snethen's article):

> *Essentials of Nursing Research* explains that the purpose of literature reviews is "to tell the reader about current knowledge on a topic and to illuminate the significance of the new study. Literature reviews are often intertwined with the problem statement as a part of the argument for the study" (Polit & Beck, 2014, p. 253). The opening paragraph of this literature review mentions how "women tend to experience a disproportionate burden of disease and poorer quality of life attributable to obesity than men" (Buxton & Snethen, 2013, p. 253). This observation strengthens the argument of the study because it verifies that women are a population that needs to be studied.

Notice how the student has integrated the quotations into his own writing, not simply dropped them into the paragraph.

Citing sources can also provide a shorthand way of summarizing the current state of knowledge. Here is an example from the paper of one of our students writing on the emotional experience of menopause:

> More than 1 million women per year begin the menopause transition, and roughly 20% of those women, or approximately 250,000 women per year, have some degree of depression during their menopause transition (Gramann et al., 2011). The results of multiple qualitative and quantitative research studies have supported the claim that the

menopause transition can be a time of increased depression and anxiety (Cohen et al., 2006; Im & Meleis, 2001; Soares, 2010; Soares & Zitek, 2007).

Notice in this case that a single parenthetical citation might include several references, each separated by a semicolon, and that they are listed in alphabetical order (which makes them easier to find in the references). Often an entire paragraph through sequential sentences and citations might synthesize the current state of knowledge, as in this example from one of our students studying caregiver stress among family members caring for an Alzheimer's patient:

> Lack of support from health care providers is one of the most significant predictors of emotional and personal strain, role overload, and role captivity among caregivers of community-dwelling patients with dementia (Diwan, Houghham, & Sachs, 2004; Gaugler et al., 2004). Caregivers of patients with Alzheimer's disease are also significantly more likely to require bereavement services after patient death than other diagnoses, and if not receiving hospice care, these bereavement needs are usually left unsupported (Jones, 2010). Moreover, nearly half of caregivers showed clinically significant levels of depression during the last few months of the patient's life, which is higher than rates of depression among caregivers of other diseases (Schulz et al., 2003). Lower level of satisfaction with social supports is significantly also associated with post-loss depression among caregivers (Burton et al., 2008). Finally, caregiver burden is one of the top two reasons for institutionalization of patients with dementia, which is associated with lower quality of life for the patient (Volicer, Hurley, & Blasi, 2003; Waldemar et al., 2007).

Notice in this example that the strategic use of transitional words like *also, moreover,* and *finally* guides the reader through this dense summary and demonstrates the way that the writer has integrated and synthesized disparate sources into a coherent whole. For more on such transitional words—also called *linking words* or *signposts*—see Chapter 9.

How to Cite Sources in APA Style

Citing and documenting sources (i.e., showing readers when you have used external sources and showing them where that material has come from) is important for two reasons. The first is legal and ethical: failing to cite sources and to use verbatim quotations or paraphrases correctly opens you up to the charge of plagiarism, which can earn you a failing grade in a course or disciplinary action in your career. The second is rhetorical: carefully citing sources shows you to be a credible, competent, and diligent reader of the evidence base. It also signals your membership in the field. Conversely, disregarding standard documentation marks you as an outsider.

Nursing researchers and journals use the *Publication Manual of the American Psychological Association* (APA, 2010) to format papers, including citations and references. There are other alternatives that nurse researchers sometimes use, including American Medical Association (AMA) style and Vancouver style, both of which use numbered in-text citations with corresponding numbered references that are arranged in the order in which they first appear in the manuscript. However, there are two advantages to APA style. First, by adopting a style guide developed by social sciences, nurse researchers signal their commitment to interdisciplinary research that includes quantitative, qualitative, and mixed methods. Historically, APA style may have become dominant because the first generation of doctorally prepared nurse faculty earned their degrees in the social sciences (that is, before nursing schools developed their own doctoral programs). Second, by providing an author's last name and the year of publication, APA style allows readers to recognize the source without having to flip to notes at the end of the paper.

In APA style, sources are cited through an *in-text parenthetical citation* with a corresponding bibliographic entry in a section called *References* at the end of the paper. The two documentation components, then, are the in-text citation and the reference for each work. The format is roughly the same for these regardless of the type of source:

> *In-text parenthetical citation*: (Last name, Year).

> *Reference*: Last name, Initials. (Year). Title. Publishing information.

Some technical differences appear depending on the number of authors, the type of authors (named individuals or corporate authors), and the type of publication. You can place the in-text citations in one of two ways: either by naming the author(s) in a sentence, immediately followed by the parenthetical citation of the year of publication, or by inserting the parenthetical citation with author(s) and year at the end of the sentence. For example, in citing a mixed-methods study conducted by Cheryl Beck and Robert Gable, published in 2012, you could write either:

> According to Beck and Gable (2012), a significant percentage of labor and delivery nurses assisting in traumatic births experience a form of post-traumatic stress known as *secondary PTSD*.

or

> A significant percentage of labor and delivery nurses assisting in traumatic births experience a form of post-traumatic stress known as *secondary PTSD* (Beck & Gable, 2012).

Notice that the word *and* appears in the naming of the authors when they are part of the sentence, but the ampersand symbol (*&*) appears when the names are placed within an in-text parenthetical citation.

The reference for that article at the end of the paper looks like this:

> Beck, C. T., & Gable, R. K. (2012). A mixed methods study of secondary traumatic stress labor and delivery nurses. *Journal of Obstetric, Gynecologic, and Neonatal Nursing, 41,* 747–760.

Citations and References by Type of Author

Here are some common versions, with the in-text citation followed by the reference for each.

For a single author:

> *In-text citation*: According to Beck (1996) . . . or . . . (Beck, 1996).

>> *Reference*: Beck, C. T. (1996). Postpartum depressed mothers' experiences interacting with their children. *Nursing Research, 45,* 98–104.

For two authors:

> *In-text citation*: Telford and Long (2012) observe that . . . or . . . (Telford & Long, 2012).

>> *Reference*: Telford, J. C., & Long, T. L. (2012). Gendered spaces, gendered pages: Union women in Civil War nurse narratives. *Medical Humanities, 38*(2), 97–105. doi:10.1136/medhum-2012-010195

For three, four, or five authors:

> *In-text citation* (first citation): According to Beck, Driscoll, and Watson (2013) ... or ... (Beck, Driscoll, & Watson, 2013).

> *In-text citation* (second and all subsequent citations): Beck et al. (2013) observe that ... or ... (Beck et al., 2013).

> > *Reference*: Beck, C. T., Driscoll, J. W., & Watson, S. (2013). *Traumatic childbirth*. New York: Routledge.

For six or more authors:

> *In-text citation*: Long et al. (2012) describe ... or ... (Long et al., 2012).

> > *Reference*: Long, T. L., et al. (2012). Competence and care: Signature pedagogies in nursing education. In N. L. Chick, A. Haynie, & R. A. R. Gurung (Eds.). *Exploring more signature pedagogies: Approaches to teaching disciplinary habits of mind* (pp. 171–187). Sterling, VA, Stylus Publishing.

Although we are accustomed to thinking of an author as an individual human being, corporate authorship is also common, especially in the production and publication of reports and policy papers.

For groups with a well-known abbreviation:

> *In-text citation* (first citation): According to the Institute of Medicine (IOM, 2011) ... or ... (Institute of Medicine [IOM], 2011).

> *In-text citation* (second and subsequent citations): The IOM (2011) recommends that ... or ... (IOM, 2011).

> > *Reference*: Institute of Medicine (IOM). (2011). *The future of nursing: Leading change, advancing health.* Washington, DC: National Academies Press.

For groups with no common abbreviation (and no publication date):

> *In-text citation*: University of Connecticut School of Nursing (n.d.) ... or ... (University of Connecticut School of Nursing, n.d.)

>> *Reference*: University of Connecticut School of Nursing. (n.d.) Center for Nursing Scholarship. Retrieved from http://nursing.uconn.edu/research/center-nursing-scholarship-cns

Notice that in this example the web page cited has no copyright date, so the abbreviation *n.d.* is used in place of a year of publication. The lack of a clear publication date is often an issue with websites.

References by Type of Publication

Although peer-reviewed journal articles are the gold standard for nursing research, books, book chapters, government documents, and official websites may also be useful and valid sources. Here we offer the formula for citing the source, followed by examples. We ask you to pay attention to some formatting issues with each example. First, notice that in each

---

How to Format a Hanging Indent in References

Microsoft Word and other word processing programs will automatically insert the hanging indent format, so please don't do it manually with a line break and tab indents. In Word, place the cursor at the beginning of the reference, click on the *Paragraph* menu, select *Indentation* and *Special:*, and then select *Hanging.*

case, the first line of the reference is flush to the left margin while each subsequent line is indented about five spaces. This is called a *hanging indent*. Notice also that book and periodical titles are *italicized*. Finally, pay attention to when and how capitalization is used (or not used).

The titles of journals use what is called *title capitalization*. The first word and any nouns and adjectives begin with capital letters. For example:

Research in Nursing and Health

or

Journal for Nurses in Professional Development

However, the titles of articles published in those journals use what is known as *sentence capitalization*, with only the first word and any proper nouns capitalized:

Gendered spaces, gendered pages: Union women in Civil War nurse narratives.

or

A mixed methods study of secondary traumatic stress labor and delivery nurses.

Book titles, although italicized like titles of periodicals, also take sentence capitalization:

AIDS and American apocalypticism: The cultural semiotics of an epidemic or

The future of nursing: Leading change, advancing health.

Note that the first word of the subtitle after the colon also begins with a capital letter.

Articles
References for journal articles include the following fields of information in this format:
Author(s). (Year of publication). Article title. *Journal title, volume* (issue number), page range.

> Beck, C. T., & Gable, R. K. (2012). A mixed methods study of secondary traumatic stress labor and delivery nurses. *Journal of Obstetric, Gynecologic, and Neonatal Nursing, 41,* 747–760.

Books and Chapters in Books
References for books include the following fields of information in this format:
Author(s). (Year of publication). *Book title.* City: Publisher.

> Creswell, J. W., & Plano Clark, V. L. (2011). *Designing and conducting mixed methods research.* Los Angeles, CA: SAGE.

References for chapters in books include the following fields of information in this format:
Author(s). (Year of publication). Chapter title. In Editors, *Book title* (edition and page range). City: Publisher.

> Guba, E., & Lincoln, Y. (1994). Competing paradigms in qualitative research. In N. Denzin & Y. Lincoln (Eds.), *Handbook of qualitative research* (pp. 105–117). Thousand Oaks, CA: Sage.

Websites

References for online sources (which may include official government reports and statistics, policy documents, and information from health organizations) include the following fields of information in this format:

Author (usually a corporate author). (Year of publication, typically found at the bottom of the Web page). Title. City: Source. Retrieved from URL (Web address).

> American Association of Colleges of Nursing (AACN). (2010). *Recommended baccalaureate competencies and curricular guidelines for the nursing care of older adults.* Washington, DC: AACN. Retrieved from http:// www.aacn.nche.edu/geriatric-nursing/AACN_ Gerocompetencies.pdf

Guidance for Other Kinds of Sources

We have provided you with guidance for the most frequently used kinds of sources (periodical articles, books and book chapters, and websites), but there are even more kinds of sources that we do not describe here in order to provide you with a concise guide. The authoritative source for formatting APA citations and references is the most recent edition of the *Publication Manual of the American Psychological Association.* We can also recommend the APA's official style website: http://www.apastyle.org/.

References appear in a separate section at the end of a paper or book, beginning with the centered heading **References**. They are arranged in alphabetical order by the first authors' last names. If multiple works by the same author are included, they are then arranged chronologically for that author by year of publication. See the references at the end of this book for this arrangement.

REFERENCES

Aitken, L. M., & Marshall, A. P. (2007). Writing a case study: Ensuring a meaningful contribution to the literature. *Australian
Critical Care, 20,* 132–136.

American Nurses Association (ANA). (2013). Euthanasia, assisted
suicide, and aid in dying (position statement). Retrieved from
http://nursingworld.org/euthanasiaanddying.

American Psychological Association (APA). (2010). *Publication
manual of the American Psychological Association.* Washington,
DC: APA, 2010.

Baker, C. R. (1996). Reflective learning: A teaching strategy for
critical thinking. *Journal of Nursing Education, 35,* 19–22.

Barnsteiner, J. H., Reeder, V. C., Palma, W. H., Preston, A. M., &
Walton, M. K. (2010). Promoting evidence-based practice and
translational research. *Nursing Administration Quarterly,
34*(3), 217–255.

Beck, C. T. (1983). Parturients' temporal experiences during the
phases of labor. *Western Journal of Nursing Research, 5,*
283–295.

Beck, C. T. (1995). The effects of postpartum depression on maternal-
infant interaction: A meta-analysis. *Nursing Research, 44,*
298–304.

Beck, C. T. (1996). Postpartum depressed mothers' experiences
interacting with their children. *Nursing Research, 45,* 98–104.

Beck, C. T. (2004). Birth trauma: In the eye of the beholder.
Nursing Research, 53, 28–35.

Beck, C. T. (2009). An adult survivor of child sexual abuse and her
breastfeeding experience: A case study. *MCN: The American
Journal of Maternal Child Nursing, 34,* 91–97.

Beck, C. T. (2014). *Postpartum mood and anxiety disorders: Case studies, research, and nursing care.* Washington, DC: Association of Women's Health, Obstetrics, and Neonatal Nurses.

Bennett, S. (2011). Confidentiality in clinical writing: Ethical dilemmas in publishing case material from clinical social work practice. *Smith College Studies in Social Work, 81,* 7–25.

Brown, S. J. (2012). *Evidence-based nursing: The research-practice connection.* Sudbury, MA: Jones & Bartlett Learning.

Buresh, B., & Gordon, S. (2000). *From silence to voice: What nurses know and must communicate to the public.* Ottawa, Canada: Canadian Nurses Association.

Buresh, B., Gordon, S., & Bell, N. (1991). Who counts in news coverage of health care? *Nursing Outlook, 39*(5), 204–208.

CINAHL Plus. (n.d.). University of Connecticut Libraries, Storrs, CT. Retrieved from http://rdl.lib.uconn.edu/byTitle.php?search=cinahl&mode=contains.

Cohen, H. (2006). How to write a patient case report. *American Journal of Health-System Pharmacy, 63,* 1888–1982.

Copp, L. A. (1997). Reading and writing editorials. *Journal of Professional Nursing, 113*(3), 137–138.

Creswell, J. W., & Plano Clark, V. L. (2011). *Designing and conducting mixed methods research.* Los Angeles, CA: SAGE.

Cusson, R., & Alexander, I. (2014, February 21). Take reins off advanced practice nurses. *Hartford Courant.* http://www.courant.com/opinion/hc-op-cusson-alexander-health-care-changes-expand--20140221-story.html.

Epp, S. (2008). The value of reflective journaling in undergraduate nursing education: A literature review. *International Journal of Nursing Studies, 45,* 1379–1388.

Fontanarosa, P. B. (2014, June). Editorial matters: Guidelines for writing effective editorials. *Journal of the American Medical Association, 311*(21), 2179–2180.

Frawley, J., & Finney-Brown, T. (2013). Writing for publication: Case studies. *Australian Journal of Herbal Medicine, 25*(3), 138–140.

Galvan, J. L. (2014). *Writing literature reviews: A guide for students of social and behavioral science.* Glendale, CA: Pyrczak Publishing.

Gibbs, G. (1998). *Learning by doing: A guide to teaching and learning methods.* Oxford: Further Education Unit, Oxford Polytechnic.

Grady, P. A. (2010). Translational research and nursing science. *Nursing Outlook, 58*(3), 164–166.

Graham, R., Mancher, M., Wolman, D. M., Greenfield, S., & Steinberg, E. (Eds.) (2011). *Clinical practice guidelines we can trust.* Washington, DC: National Academies Press.

Guba, E., & Lincoln, Y. (1994). Competing paradigms in qualitative research. In N. Denzin & Y. Lincoln (Eds.), *Handbook of qualitative research* (pp. 105–117). Thousand Oaks, CA: Sage.

INANE Predatory Publishing Practices Collective. (2014). Predatory publishing: What editors need to know. *Nurse Author and Editor, 24*(3). Retrieved from http://www.nurseauthoreditor.com/tocs.asp?yr=2014&num=3.

Juyal, D., Thaledi, S., & Thawani, V. (2013). Writing patient case reports for publication. *Education for Health, 26*(2), 126–129.

Lewis, L. F. (2015). Caregiving for a loved one with dementia at the end of life: An emergent theory of rediscovering. *American Journal of Alzheimer's Disease and Other Dementia, 30,* 488–496.

Linder, L. (2012). Disseminating research and scholarly projects: Developing a successful abstract. *Journal of Pediatric Oncology Nursing, 29*(6), 362–366.

Ling Pan, M. (2013). *Preparing literature reviews: Qualitative and quantitative approaches.* Glendale, CA: Pyrczak Publishing.

Long, T. L. (2005). *AIDS and American apocalypticism: The cultural semiotics of an epidemic*. Albany, NY: State University of New York Press.

McGrath, J. M. (2012). Systematic and integrative reviews of the literature: How are they changing our thoughts about practice? *Journal of Perinatal & Neonatal Nursing, 26*, 193–195.

Melnyk, B. M., & Fineout-Overholt, E. (2011). *Evidence-based practice in nursing and healthcare*. Philadelphia, PA: Wolters Kluwer Health/Lippincott Williams and Wilkins.

Mezirow, I. (1981). A critical theory of adult learning and education. *Adult Education, 32*(1), 3–24.

National Library of Medicine. (1999, 2014). *Medical subject headings*. Retrieved from http://www.nlm.nih.gov/mesh/.

Nigliazzo, S. (2015, July 28). Nursing and writing roundtable: Part 1. *Bellevue Literary Review*. Retrieved from http://blr.med.nyu .edu/news/2015/roundtable-discussion-close-observation-the -skills-nursing-and-writing.

Oermann, M., & Hays, J. C. (2010). *Writing for publication in nursing* (2nd ed.) New York: Springer Publishing.

Patton, M. Q. (1990). *Qualitative evaluation and research methods*. Newbury Park, CA: Sage Publications.

Polit, D. F., & Beck, C. T. (2010). Generalization in quantitative and qualitative research: Myths and strategies. *International Journal of Nursing Studies, 47*, 1451–1458.

Polit, D. F., & Beck, C. T. (2017). *Nursing research: Generating and assessing evidence for nursing practice*. Philadelphia, PA: Wolters Kluwer.

Polit, D. F., & Beck, C. T. (2014). *Essentials of nursing research: Appraising evidence for nursing practice*. Philadelphia, PA: Wolters Kluwer.

Powell, J. H. (1989). The reflective practitioner in nursing. *Journal of Advanced Nursing, 14*, 824–832.

PubMed. (n.d.). University of Connecticut Libraries, Storrs, CT. http://rdl.lib.uconn.edu/byTitle.php?search=pubmed&mode=contains

Sackett, D. L., Straus, S. E., Richardson, W. S., Rosenberg, W., & Haynes, R. B. (2000). *Evidence-based medicine: How to practice and teach EBM*. London: Churchill Livingstone.

Sandelowski, M. (2008). Tables or tableaux? The challenges of writing and reading mixed methods studies. In V. L. Plano Clark & J. W. Creswell (Eds.), *The mixed methods reader* (pp. 301–336). Los Angeles, CA: SAGE.

Saver, C. (2011). *Anatomy of writing for publication for nurses*. Indianapolis, IN: Sigma Theta Tau International.

Selikoff, I. J. (1991). Asbestos disease 1990–2020: The risks of asbestos risk assessment. *Toxicology and Industrial Health, 7*, 117–126.

Singh, A., & Singh, S. (2006). What is a good editorial? *Mens Sana Monograph, 4*(1), 14–17.

Stevens, K. (2013, May 31). The impact of evidence-based practice in nursing and the next big ideas. *OJIN: The Online Journal of Issues in Nursing, 18*(2), Manuscript 4. Retrieved from http://nursingworld.org/MainMenuCategories/ANAMarketplace/ANAPeriodicals/OJIN/TableofContents/Vol-18-2013/No2-May-2013/Impact-of-Evidence-Based-Practice.html.

Tashakkori, A., & Creswell, J. (2007). The new era of mixed methods. *Journal of Mixed Methods Research, 1*, 3–7.

Titler, M. G. (2010). Translation science and context. *Resource and Theory for Nursing Practice: An International Journal, 24*(1), 35–55.

Usher, K., Tollefson, J., & Francis, D. (2001). Moving from technical to critical reflection in journaling: An investigation of students' ability to incorporate three levels of reflective writing. *Australian Journal of Advanced Nursing, 19*(1), 15–19.

CREDITS

Page 48, *Figure 2.1*: Adapted from Polit and Beck (2014, p. 23), by
permission of Wolters Kluwer Health.

Page 139, *Table 8.2*: Adapted from U.S. Department of Labor Bureau of
Labor Statistics, Occupational Employment and Wages, May 2014,
29-1141 Registered Nurses. Retrieved from http://www.bls.gov/oes/
current/oes291141.htm#st.

Page 140, *Figure 8.2*: Data were provided by the National League for Nursing,
www.nln.org/research/slides/index.htm.

Page 140, *Figure 8.3*: Data were provided by the National League for
Nursing (2013), Annual Survey of Schools of Nursing, Fall 2012,
www.nln.org/research/slides/index.htm.

Page 141, *Figure 8.4*: Data were provided by the National League for Nursing,
www.nln.org/research/slides/index.htm.

Page 149, *Figure 8.11*: Courtesy of the UConn School of Nursing.

INDEX